# SWEAT AND BLOOD

# SWEAT AND BLOOD

## A HISTORY OF U.S. LABOR UNIONS

GLORIA SKURZYNSKI

TWENTY-FIRST CENTURY BOOKS · MINNEAPOLIS

## FOR KATELIN MARIE THOMPSON. WELCOME TO THE WORLD.

For their advice on the contents of this book, the author
wishes to thank Dr. Curtis Miner, Senior Curator of History,
The State Museum of Pennsylvania, Harrisburg, PA, and Dr.
Wilson J. Warren, Associate Professor, History Department,
Western Michigan University, Kalamazoo, Michigan.

Twenty-First Century Books
A division of Lerner Publishing Group, Inc.
241 First Avenue North
Minneapolis, MN 55401 U.S.A.

Website address: www.lernerbooks.com

Library of Congress Cataloging-in-Publication Data

Skurzynski, Gloria.
    Sweat and blood : a history of U.S. labor unions / by
    Gloria Skurzynski.
        p.    cm. — (People's history)
    Includes bibliographical references and index.
    ISBN 978-0-8225-7594-8 (lib. bdg. : alk. paper)
    1. Labor unions—United States—History—Juvenile
literature.  2. Working class—United States—History—
Juvenile literature.  I. Title.
    HD6508.S545  2009
    331.880973—dc22                          2007050270

Manufactured in the United States of America
1  2  3  4  5  6  –  BP  –  14  13  12  11  10  09

# CONTENTS

# CHAPTER ONE

# IN THE BEGINNING

In order to form a more perfect union." Near the end of the 1700s, members of the first Continental Congress used that phrase to unite thirteen states into one American nation. Two centuries later in the United States, the word *union* had come to mean the alliance of tens of millions of American men and women, union members who'd fought together to win safe working conditions, decent pay, health benefits, the right to work at whatever jobs they wanted, and many additional rights.

When the American colonies were brand new, workers had no protection against unfair masters who might treat them harshly. Working every day (except Sunday, in some cases) from dawn to sunset for meager pay, they struggled to earn enough to feed and clothe their families. Some of the workers, called indentured servants, received no pay at all.

In the 1600s and 1700s, if free persons wanted to come to the American colonies but couldn't afford to pay for passage on a ship, they could sell themselves to the ship's captain. After the ship reached port in the colonies, the captain would resell these people as indentured servants. Neither slave nor free, indentured servants had to work without wages as payment for their passage. If they had skills such as weaving or carpentry, the term of their indenture might be five years. If they were unskilled, the term would be longer, probably seven years. The need for laborers in the American colonies was so great that prisoners awaiting the death penalty in England could be pardoned if they agreed to emigrate from England to the American continent as indentured servants. As many as sixty thousand British convicts were transported to the American colonies before the American Revolution (1775–1783).

Indentured servants lived under the total control of the person who bought them. They had no freedom and no rights until their indenture ended—if they survived until then. The death rate was high. As many as half of the indentured servants in the American colonies died during their first two years in their new home. But indentured servants who had completed their terms could begin life over again as free men and women.

Laborers who wanted to go to the American colonies but could not afford to would often sign a contract of indenture *(above)*.

With freedom came the desire for control. Many immigrants learned new skills in America. Some learned them while they paid off their terms of indenture. Others gained skills serving as apprentices to masters of the trade and learning from them in the bustling colonial economy. When particular skills were desperately needed, the workers who had those skills could make demands—and win.

## AN EARLY VICTORY

The first case of worker power in colonial America took place at the beginning of the 1600s in Jamestown, Virginia. The settlement needed skilled workers, so Captain John Smith, its leader, invited a small group of craftsmen to join the Jamestown colonists. At least four who arrived came from Poland. The Poles were the only Catholics in this Protestant colony, but the religious difference was tolerated because their skills were so badly needed. One of the Polish glassworkers wrote, "First of all we set up a sawmill, cutting beams and planks without respite. Also without wasting any time, we built a glasshouse . . . and began blowing glasses, bottles, jugs, as well as beads, for which the Virginia female Indians brought us grain and fish in their baskets, picking up every chip of glass from the ground to decorate their strange attire."

Settlers land in Jamestown, Virginia. As depicted in this seventeenth-century English painting, the majority of the settlers in Jamestown were English and Protestant. A few of the craftsmen who were brought to the colony were Catholic and Polish.

In 1619 Virginia formed a government and the citizens of Jamestown elected representatives to their governing body, which was called the House of Burgesses. The Polish workers were denied the right to vote. Because of this, the Poles refused to work—the first documented labor strike in America. It got results. From London, English officials (who ruled the American colonies) reacted hastily with a directive recorded in the Virginia Court Book of July 21, 1619. It reads:

> "They shall be enfranchised [allowed to vote], and made as free as any inhabitant there whatsoever; And because their skill . . . shall not dye [die] with them, it is agreed that some young men, shall be put unto them to learn their skill and knowledge herein for the benefit of the Country hereafter."

America's first workers' strike was a success.

## READY TO REVOLT

European merchants had a centuries-long tradition of joining together to form guilds. The guilds protected their members from rulers who demanded payment for allowing merchants to trade in their lands.

The merchants traded goods produced by skilled workers. Soon these skilled workers formed guilds of their own. Craftsmen's guilds decided the prices, the quality, and the amount of goods they would produce. Weavers, dyers, blacksmiths, armor makers, jewelers, glassmakers, and many other skilled workers formed their own craft guilds. They called themselves guildsmen. They met in guildhalls, where they were ranked as masters, journeymen, or apprentices, according to their experience.

Masters owned shops where they trained apprentices. The apprentices usually received room and board but no pay. The apprenticeship might last for many years. When the apprentices finally finished their training, they were called journeymen. Journeymen could try to reach the rank of master, but the number of masters in each guild was limited—by the masters themselves. If masters wanted to, they could prevent their journeymen from ever working independently.

## WAR AND REVOLUTION

Over time, it became harder for craftsmen to be accepted into guilds unless they were the sons or relatives of the masters. Guilds resisted change, but change kept happening all around them. By the late 1700s, many goods were produced in European factories rather than by skilled guildsmen. This was the beginning of the Industrial Revolution. Factory owners would hire anyone, skilled or unskilled, who could handle a job. Guilds were abolished in France during the French Revolution (1789–1799), a war that overthrew that nation's royal rulers. Revolutionary leaders viewed guilds as part of "a society based on privilege."

In the American colony of Pennsylvania, in the year 1770, a guild called the Carpenters' Company of the City and County of Philadelphia (the oldest trade guild in America) finished building its guildhall on Chestnut Street. It was an imposing two-story structure with a steeple. Here, in the Carpenters' Hall, the delegates to the First Continental Congress met on September 5, 1774. They drew up a list of the American colonies' grievances against Great Britain's King George III.

Revolution was in the air. As American revolutionaries fought for their independence from Britain, workers were inspired to find ways to improve their own working conditions. In 1778, in New York City, for example, journeyman printers united to demand an increase in wages. They received what they asked for but then disbanded.

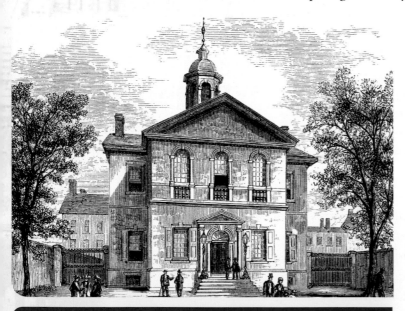

This nineteenth-century American illustration shows Carpenters' Hall in Philadelphia, Pennsylvania. Carpenters' Hall was built by members of the Carpenters' Company, the oldest guild in the United States.

According to historian Marcus Rediker, the word *strike*, meaning "to refuse to work," came from British sailors. In a labor dispute, they "struck their sails" (lowered the sails of their vessels) to keep from sailing. In 1786 a print shop owner in Philadelphia tried to reduce the wages of skilled print craftsmen to $5.83 per week. Twenty-six Philadelphia printers threatened to "not engage to work for any printing establishment in this city or county under the sum of $6.00 per week." They won a minimum $6.00 weekly wage. But in 1791, when Philadelphia carpenters—who worked from sunup to sundown—struck for a ten-hour working day, that strike failed.

In 1792 Philadelphia shoemakers formed one of the first unions for collective bargaining. This form of negotiation over working conditions takes place between organized workers and their employers. The shoemakers didn't actually call themselves a union—the term hadn't yet come into use. They didn't use the term *guild*, either. Instead, they called their organization a society. After a year or so, the shoemakers grew discouraged and the group disbanded. In 1794 they tried organizing again, this time naming themselves the Federal Society of Journeymen Cordwainers (FSJC). (A cordwainer made shoes from cordovan, a kind of leather.) Over the next ten years, they managed to gain a few small wage increases from their employers. Their real success came in forcing Philadelphia shoe manufacturers to hire only members of the FSJC.

## CLOSED SHOP

A workplace where the owners must employ only union members, through choice or through an agreement with the unions, is called a closed shop. Manufacturers dislike closed shops because it means they can't hire workers willing to work for wages lower than those set by the union.

In 1805, when FSJC members struck for even higher wages, eight of their leaders were arrested and brought to trial. They were accused of violating the English Common Law of Conspiracy (plotting in secret). Philadelphia patriots had been a major force in the battle against Great Britain for U.S. independence. So it seemed strange for prosecutors to use a law from Great Britain against the FSJC. Defense lawyers pointed this out, telling the jury, "If you are desirous of introducing a similar [to the British] spirit of inequality into our government and laws . . . if you think that the labourer and the journeyman enjoy too great a portion of liberty . . . then [such faulty] opinions will lead you to convict the defendants." The prosecuting attorney called the strikers "transitory [not permanent], irresponsible, and dangerous." It was true that some minor fighting had taken place during the strike. One FSJC member threw a potato through a shop window. But the main complaint against the FSJC was that it prevented manufacturers from hiring nonmembers. The prosecution stated, speaking about nonunion workers, "The Society [FSJC] has no right to force you into its body, and then say you shall obey its rules under severe penalties." After a three-day trial, the jury found the FSJC defendants guilty. They were fined eight dollars each (one week's wages). Because of this trial, labor unions were regarded as illegal conspiracies until the mid-1800s.

## SLAVERY

By the mid-1800s, about one-third of the people living in the southern states were slaves. Sold to slave owners, usually in public auctions, slaves were considered property. Slaves and their descendants belonged to owners forever. The owners' descendants inherited slaves just as they inherited land or buildings or wealth.

Slaves in the South, both parents and children, were mostly field laborers. Others worked as house servants for their owners' families. Though they had no freedom, some slaves were treated decently by their masters. Often this was not because of any sense of common humanity. Slaves were cared for in the same way owners cared for useful carriage horses or hunting dogs. Slaves were expensive to replace, so they required enough care to keep them in good working condition.

For the first two-thirds of the nineteenth century, slaves had no hope of freedom unless they ran away to the North, where slavery had been

Slaves pick cotton on a plantation in Louisiana in the 1800s.

outlawed. A former runaway slave recalled, "I have been hunted by the hounds a great many times. The only way to do when I heard them coming, was to go across water, and put them off the scent, and then climb a high tree in the thickest part of the swamp where the overseer can't come. If the hunters could see us they would shoot us. They don't think any more about shooting a [black man] than a dog. It's all one thing. I have seen several shot."

## ENGINE OF CHANGE

Cotton was the main money-producing crop in the South. Field slaves planted cotton, hoed cotton, picked cotton, and then cleaned the seeds out of the cotton balls. By hand, a slave could clean about 1 pound (0.5 kilograms) of cotton a day. With the invention of the mechanical cotton gin ("gin" is short for "engine"), a slave could clean as much as 50 pounds (23 km) of cotton in a day. This made cotton cheaper to produce and led to an increase in the number of slaves needed to work on the South's cotton plantations.

By this time, Samuel Slater in Rhode Island had developed a cotton-spinning machine that ran on water power. It was based on a British

This illustration from a periodical of the 1800s shows slaves using a cotton gin to clean cotton. The cotton gin made cotton cheaper and raised the demand for slave labor to grow and clean even more cotton.

invention. Factories in the northeastern United States used power looms to weave cotton fabric. Cotton brought from the South could be carded, spun, and woven all in the same factory. Because factories produced cotton cloth more quickly and cheaply, more people could buy it. Factories needed more raw cotton to meet the demand for cloth, so the cotton growers needed more slaves to produce it.

The cycle kept spiraling upward—larger crops, more slaves, and additional factories turning out even more cotton cloth more cheaply for buyers eager to purchase it. In 1826 northern textile mills created 37 million yards (34 million meters) of cloth. By 1856 the mills were producing 775 million yards (708 million m).

The growth of factories in the North meant more employees were needed to work them. Americans left their farms for these factory jobs. Farm income depended on good weather and successful harvests. In some years, crops failed and families earned no money. So country people— not only men but women and children too—came to towns to work for more dependable factory wages. Working conditions could be harsh, and the workers had little power to improve them. When labor unions promised to fight for workers' rights, Americans began to heed the call to organize.

ONE OF THE GIRLS . . . [GAVE] A NEAT SPEECH, DECLARING THAT IT WAS THEIR DUTY TO RESIST ALL ATTEMPTS AT CUTTING DOWN THE WAGES. THIS WAS THE FIRST TIME A WOMAN HAD SPOKEN IN PUBLIC IN LOWELL [MASSACHUSETTS], AND THE EVENT CAUSED SURPRISE AND CONSTERNATION.

—FACTORY WORKER HARRIET HANSON ROBINSON, 1898, QUOTED IN *LOOM AND SPINDLE*

# SETTLERS AND IMMIGRANTS

Boys and girls raised on farms usually climbed out of bed at sunrise. They worked in the fields raising crops that later appeared on their own family's dinner table. Without electricity, farm families followed the cycle of seasons and sunlight to do their chores. They worked hard during the daylight hours in spring, summer, and autumn, planting, cultivating, and harvesting their crops. There was less to do in winter when the growing season was over.

When those boys and girls left farms and went to the city to work in factories, life changed drastically. The factory bell rang out before sunrise, as early as four in the morning, to start the day. There was no morning meal with family gathered around the table—no family at all. In the factory, there were only strangers standing side by side next to clattering, vibrating machinery. Each worker labored for ten, twelve, or even fourteen hours a day, earning barely enough to rent a room to sleep in and to buy food to eat. Outside, seasons changed, but inside everything stayed the same from one year to the next. Every motion was repeated endlessly as cotton and wool were spun, boots were sewn, or metal was shaped into tools. An injury at work—which was common—meant loss of the job, with no help from the factory owners. Someone was always eagerly waiting to fill that job. By 1840, out of a total U.S. population of 17 million, close to 800,000 men, women, and children worked in factories in the United States, particularly in the Northeast. Women earned less than men for the same kinds of jobs—often as little as $1.56 per week. Manufacturers who wanted to cut their costs even further hired prison convicts at cheaper wages. The lowest pay of all went to children as young as six. They were hired to crawl underneath the machinery to pick up anything that had fallen to the floor.

## SKILLED WORKERS ONLY

Trade unions existed during this time, but only skilled workers were allowed to join. These included carpenters, printers, mechanics, stonecutters, or cabinetmakers—not unskilled factory workers. Factory work didn't require much skill. Workers who did not have a trade found

Factory life in the United States from the 1830s into the 1900s meant long hours in cramped quarters. This northern factory produced textiles.

themselves standing in front of factory machines, repeating the same actions over and over. They performed only small steps in the manufacturing process of a product they might never even see when it was finished. Pride of workmanship vanished.

## TIME TABLE OF THE LOWELL MILLS,
### To take effect on and after Oct. 21st, 1851.

The Standard time being that of the meridian of Lowell, as shown by the regulator clock of JOSEPH RAYNES, 43 Central Street.

| | From 1st to 10th inclusive. | | | | From 11th to 20th inclusive. | | | | From 21st to last day of month. | | | |
|---|---|---|---|---|---|---|---|---|---|---|---|---|
| | 1st Bell | 2d Bell | 3d Bell | Eve. Bell | 1st Bell | 2d Bell | 3d Bell | Eve. Bell | 1st Bell | 2d Bell | 3d Bell | Eve. Bell |
| January, | 5.00 | 6.00 | 6.50 | *7.30 | 5.00 | 6.00 | 6.50 | *7.30 | 5.00 | 6.00 | 6.50 | *7.30 |
| February, | 4.30 | 5.30 | 6.40 | *7.30 | 4.30 | 5.30 | 6.25 | *7.30 | 4.30 | 5.30 | 6.15 | *7.30 |
| March, | 5.40 | 6.00 | | *7.30 | 5.20 | 5.40 | | *7.30 | 5.05 | 5.25 | | 6.35 |
| April, | 4.45 | 5.05 | | 6.45 | 4.30 | 4.50 | | 6.55 | 4.30 | 4.50 | | 7.00 |
| May, | 4.30 | 4.50 | | 7.00 | 4.30 | 4.50 | | 7.00 | 4.30 | 4.50 | | 7.00 |
| June, | " | " | | " | " | " | | " | " | " | | " |
| July, | " | " | | " | " | " | | " | " | " | | " |
| August, | " | " | | " | " | " | | " | " | " | | " |
| September, | 4.40 | 5.00 | | 6.45 | 4.50 | 5.10 | | 6.30 | 5.00 | 5.20 | | *7.30 |
| October, | 5.10 | 5.30 | | *7.30 | 5.20 | 5.40 | | *7.30 | 5.35 | 5.55 | | *7.30 |
| November, | 4.30 | 5.30 | 6.10 | *7.30 | 4.30 | 5.30 | 6.20 | *7.30 | 5.00 | 6.00 | 6.35 | *7.30 |
| December, | 5.00 | 6.00 | 6.45 | *7.30 | 5.00 | 6.00 | 6.50 | *7.30 | 5.00 | 6.00 | 6.50 | *7.30 |

\* Excepting on Saturdays from Sept. 21st to March 20th inclusive, when it is rung at 20 minutes after sunset.

### YARD GATES,
Will be opened at ringing of last morning bell, of meal bells, and of evening bells; and kept open Ten minutes.

### MILL GATES.
Commence hoisting Mill Gates, Two minutes before commencing work.

### WORK COMMENCES,
At Ten minutes after last morning bell, and at Ten minutes after bell which "rings in" from Meals.

### BREAKFAST BELLS.
During March "Ring out".........at.....7.30 a. m.........."Ring in" at 8.05 a. m.
April 1st to Sept. 20th inclusive.....at.....7.00 " " ........ " " at 7.35 " "
Sept. 21st to Oct. 31st inclusive.....at.....7.30 " " ........ " " at 8.05 " "
Remainder of year work commences after Breakfast.

### DINNER BELLS.
"Ring out"...... ...... ...... ...... 12.30 p. m........."Ring in".... 1.05 p. m.

In all cases, the *first* stroke of the bell is considered as marking the time.

This sign, posted at the Lowell mills in Massachusetts, set the eating and working times of the people who lived and worked at the mills. In 1851 factory workers were working more than eleven hours a day.

## TROUBLE AT THE LOOMS

A number of textile factories operated in Lowell, Massachusetts. Young women who had left farms to work in these factories lived in boardinghouses right next to the mills. They marched to work before dawn and returned to their rooms after dark. The success of the first mills led to the opening of more mills and an increase in textile production. So much cloth was being made that prices dropped. (When too much of any product is available for sale, the manufacturers lower prices to attract more buyers.)

Because of decreasing profits, Lowell's millowners cut wages in 1834. They also ordered the women to work longer and faster and to pay more rent. In response, a few of the bolder young women convinced others to go on strike. But with sales declining, a walkout by a group of workers didn't cause a problem for the owners, and the workers were not successful in their strike.

Two years later, in October 1836, the board of directors of Lowell's textile mills raised the rents in the company's boardinghouses. In response, the female textile workers organized a Factory Girls' Association and began to strike against the millowners. More than fifteen hundred workers walked off their jobs and stayed away for several weeks until the rent hike was dropped.

Victory was sweet, but it didn't last long. In the following year, 1837, a depression hit. Many of the workers lost their jobs in the weakening economy. The depression of 1837 was one of the nation's worst.

## GO WEST, YOUNG MAN

"Go West, young man, and grow up with the country." This was the title of an editorial by John B. L. Soule in the *Terre Haute [IN] Daily Express* in 1851. As the boundaries of the United States expanded in the 1800s through land purchase and war, settlers followed. It was not only the adventure of reaching new territories that attracted settlers, it was the land itself. Millions of acres could be farmed, ranched, hunted, and mined. It wasn't long before competition from cheap agricultural products grown in the new western territories began to hurt farmers in the East. They couldn't grow crops as cheaply, and facing financial ruin, many eastern farmers left their land. They moved to cities to find jobs

In the mid-1800s, settlers in the midwestern United States could harvest wheat efficiently thanks to the invention of the McCormick reaper *(above)*. They also had more land than farmers who stayed in the East.

This child is sewing the toes onto stockings in a hosiery mill. Children as young as six worked in factories throughout the 1800s and early 1900s. Starting in the 1850s, different states passed laws prohibiting children under a certain age from working in factories.

in factories. Working conditions were harsh, but workingmen did have a weapon—the vote. (Women could not yet legally vote.) They could—and did—threaten to vote for candidates who supported workingmen's issues, such as a ten-hour working day. The shorter workday became law in some states. In Pennsylvania in 1848, for example, voters passed a ten-hour law for all cotton, woolen, silk, paper, bagging, and flax factories. The new law also prohibited hiring children younger than twelve. New Jersey voters passed similar laws in 1851. In 1852 Ohio forbade hiring children under fourteen for factory work.

## CIVIL WAR

In the mid-1800s, tensions mounted over the legality of slavery in the Unites States. It was the main issue in the presidential campaign of 1860. In that year, one of the presidential candidates made a speech to shoe factory workers who had gone on strike in New Haven, Connecticut. He said, "I am glad to see that a system of labor prevails in New England [the states in the northeastern United States] under which laborers can strike when they want to, where they are not obliged to labor whether you pay them or not. I like the system that lets a man quit when he wants to, and wish it might prevail everywhere. One of the reasons I am opposed to slavery is right here." The candidate's name was Abraham Lincoln, and he won the election.

The Civil War (1861–1865) pitted the Union (the Northern, anti-slavery states) against the Confederacy (the South). The Confederacy was made up of eleven slaveholding Southern states that formally seceded (withdrew) from the United States.

Wars require supplies. The North already had far more industry than the South. New York and Pennsylvania each had more industry than all the Confederate states combined. As the war unfolded, even more Northern factories were built. They produced guns and ammunition, uniforms and boots, wagons, telegraph wires, and railroad tracks—plus many other products to supply the Union army.

Wars also require men to serve in the military. During the Civil War, many workingmen left their factory jobs to join the Union army. In fact,

Women workers fill cartridges for Northern soldiers during the Civil War. This engraving is based on a work by American artist Winslow Homer (1836–1910).

about one-third of all factory workers in the North enlisted. After President Lincoln issued the Emancipation Proclamation, freeing slaves in the Southern states, thousands of freed slaves came north to fill these jobs. The African Americans were willing to work for lower pay than the workers they replaced. This angered Northern workers. They worried that factory owners would lower pay for all workers.

## NEW AMERICANS

Among the Northerners who resented African American workers were recent immigrants. In the 1800s, they had come to the United States from all over the world, fleeing poverty and famine. Large numbers came from Italy, Ireland, and Germany.

The resentment led to anger and to violence. Beginning on Sunday, June 12, 1863, a protest mob in New

This drawing shows the burning of a government building during the 1863 draft riots in New York. Mobs protested unfair draft laws, which turned into protests over unemployment and race relations.

York City—with many Irish immigrants—looted stores and attacked African American citizens. They set fire to an African American church and orphanage and to a government office. The riot had started as a protest against unfair draft laws. (Wealthy men could pay to avoid serving in the military.) It drifted into a racial battle over jobs and employment as well. The U.S. Army was called in to restore order, but according to an officer, "The military and the police force . . . were overwhelmed and dispersed." Although no actual count was made, as many as one hundred people may have died.

The U.S. Army did put down other strikes that took place during the Civil War. These included a strike by a gun-workers union in New York, a strike by train engineers and miners in Pennsylvania, and strikes by other labor associations elsewhere.

At this time, local trade organizations began for the first time to reach out to others like themselves throughout the country. They joined with unions in other states to form national associations of workers. The struggle for workers' rights would become increasingly violent, however, as the century unfolded.

> IF YOU THINK THAT BY HANGING US YOU CAN STAMP OUT THE LABOR MOVEMENT . . . THE MOVEMENT FROM WHICH THE DOWNTRODDEN MILLIONS, . . . WHO TOIL IN WANT AND MISERY EXPECT SALVATION—IF THIS IS YOUR OPINION, THEN HANG US! HERE YOU WILL TREAD UPON A SPARK, BUT . . . EVERYWHERE, FLAMES BLAZE UP.
>
> —AUGUST SPIES, LABOR LEADER, TO JUDGE JOSEPH E. GARY, 1886

# CHAPTER THREE

# FIRE IN THE HOLE

To meet the need for increased production during the Civil War, American factories mechanized with the help of new technology. For example, gasoline engines and electricity increased efficiency along the line. This meant that fewer workers were needed to run the machinery. The end of the war in 1865 was followed by an economic slump. The number of jobs declined, while the number of workers rose because of recent immigration and soldiers released from military service.

By 1865 more than 35,000 miles (56,000 km) of railroad tracks had been laid in the United States. That number would increase fivefold in the next twenty-five years as the nation continued to expand. By mid-1866, nearly fifteen thousand Chinese laborers were building railroads in California. The Chinese workers often replaced workers who had walked off the job to hunt for gold in California, where it had been discovered in 1849. One historian said about the Chinese, "They were experts in the use of gunpowder [for blasting through rock] since it was a Chinese invention. They drank a cup of tea two or three times a day, then went right back to work. At the end of the day, their portion of track was longer and straighter than the white crews. They also worked for less money."

Yet the Chinese workers took part in a massive strike in June 1867. Five thousand Chinese workers struck the Central Pacific Railroad, demanding shorter hours and an increase in their monthly wage of thirty-five dollars. They first asked for forty dollars a month and then forty-five dollars. The railroad bosses cut off their food supplies and sent a posse, a group of volunteer lawmen, to intimidate the Chinese. The starving strikers returned to work—with no change in hours or salary. An observer named Charles Crocker said, "If there had been that number of whites in a strike, there would have been murder, drunkenness and disorder. . . . But with the Chinese, it was just like Sunday. . . . No violence was perpetrated along the whole [railroad] line."

Chinese railroad workers ride on a handcar in California. Chinese laborers were responsible for laying much of the track in California in the 1800s.

# THE MOLLY MAGUIRES

Labor violence did happen in other places, such as eastern Pennsylvania. Thousands of Irish immigrants had settled there to work in the region's coal mines. The mines had only one entrance and usually lacked proper ventilation. Some tunnel ceilings were so low the miners couldn't stand up straight. If a fire started or the mine caved in and the entrance became blocked, miners could be trapped inside. During one seven-year period, 566 miners were killed in mine accidents and 1,665 others were injured.

Workdays in the mines were long—ten to twelve hours of digging and shoveling. The shafts were dirty, dangerous, and often damp. Twenty thousand Pennsylvania miners went on strike for a shorter workday in 1868. The strike failed. The poor striking workers couldn't hold out against the resources of the wealthy, powerful mineowners. The miners then formed a union, the Workingmen's Benevolent Association (WBA). The WBA called for peaceful negotiations with mineowners. The association managed to gain a few small wage increases for the members, but the increases hardly kept up with the rising cost of living.

A group of militant Irish immigrants believed the union's peaceful, nonviolent policy was useless. They preached that only threats, beatings, sabotage, and even murder could get them what they wanted. Their secret society, called the Molly Maguires, was founded in Ireland. (Molly Maguire may have been a fierce young woman who led men through the Irish countryside on nighttime raids against the ruling British.) Molly Maguires in Pennsylvania attacked mine bosses and strikebreakers alike. Fighting back, the mineowners hired equally brutal spies from the Pinkerton National Detective Agency. They sneaked into the ranks of the Molly Maguires to gather evidence against them. After the Pinkertons turned over to the mine bosses whatever evidence they claimed to have uncovered, dozens of Molly Maguires were tried for murder and assault. Were they guilty, or were many of the alleged crimes set up by the Pinkertons themselves? No one really knows. But some people believed that at least some of the evidence was faked. Pennsylvania historian Harold Aurand

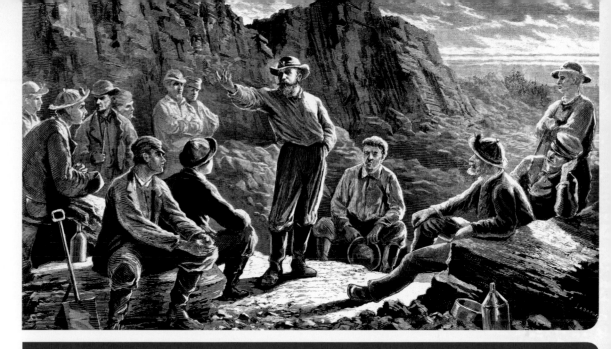

Molly Maguires meet in Pennsylvania in 1874. These miners used violence against mineowners to try to win shorter workdays and higher pay. These attempts failed, and nineteen Molly Maguires were hanged for murder and assault in 1877.

wrote, "A private police force arrested the alleged defenders, and private attorneys for the coal companies prosecuted them. The state provided only the courtroom and the gallows." Nineteen Molly Maguires were hanged, ten of them on June 21, 1877. This date was remembered by union members as Black Thursday.

## WORKING ON THE RAILROAD

About this same time, even greater violence erupted among striking railroad workers, not only in Pennsylvania but in other states as well. After the Baltimore & Ohio Railroad (B&O) cut employees' wages for the second time in a year, railroad workers went on strike in West Virginia, where the B&O had many routes. West Virginia's governor ordered the state militia to fire on the strikers. The militia refused. The strike spread to Baltimore, Maryland. There, outnumbered federal troops did fire on the strikers, killing eleven and wounding forty.

Violence was even worse in Pittsburgh, Pennsylvania. The owner of the Pennsylvania Railroad declared that strikers should be given "a rifle diet for a few days and see how they like that kind of bread." Local police refused to shoot at the strikers. The Pennsylvania state militia did shoot, killing twenty. Angry strikers chased the militiamen into a railroad depot and set fire to it.

The workers' fury spread west. Striking railroad workers in Illinois, Missouri, Michigan, and other states stopped trains on the tracks. *Harper's Magazine* reported, "Hardly a [rail]road was running, from the Hudson [River] to the Mississippi [River], and from Canada to Virginia."

In the summer of 1877 in Chicago, Illinois, violence erupted between police and the crowds, where twenty thousand people joined demonstrations in support of the striking workers. Newspaper headlines blared, "TERROR REIGNS, STREETS OF CHICAGO GIVEN OVER TO HOWLING MOBS OF THIEVES AND CUTTHROATS."

Demonstrators joined striking workers to fight against the police during the Great Railroad Strike of 1877 in Chicago.

## THE RADICALS

In the 1880s, a new labor organization pasted up notices.

WORKING MEN OF CHICAGO!

HAVE YOU NO RIGHTS?—NO AMBITION?

—NO MANHOOD?

Was it in vain that our forefathers died for LIBERTY?

Throughout the land our brothers are calling upon us

to rise and protect our Labor.

For the sake of our wives and children,

and our own self-respect,

LET US WAIT NO LONGER!

ORGANIZE AT ONCE!

MASS MEETING . . . TONIGHT!

—The Committee, Workingmen's Party of the United States.

This new labor organization had formed only recently in Philadelphia. It was strongly influenced by recent German immigrants to the United States. These Germans believed in the communistic ideas of German philosopher Karl Marx (1818–1883). Marx wrote, "There will always be a class which will exploit and a class which will be exploited."

Anarchism, Communism, and Socialism—in the 1880s, these new political philosophies were still evolving. Though they are three distinct ideologies, they often connect or overlap. Anarchism mainly favors doing away with all governments. Communism calls for a classless society in which all property is owned by the community as a whole. All people enjoy equal social and economic status. As a political movement, Communism seeks to overthrow capitalism (a system of private ownership) through a workers' revolution and to put the wealth into the hands of the proletariat, or working class.

Socialism is the belief that human society can and should be organized for the benefit of all, rather than for the profit of a few. Like Communism, it supports state ownership of the means of production (factories, farms, and businesses) but doesn't call for a worker's revolution.

At the time, Socialism was a popular idea for working-class people who felt they lacked the power to overcome capitalists, such as the factory owners. Middle- and upper-class people in the United States considered all three philosophies extremely radical.

In the United States, the Workingmen's Party became the Socialist Labor Party. It campaigned for an eight-hour day for workers. Its members urged an end to capitalism by force if necessary, a tactic encouraged by anarchists. In 1885 one of the Socialist Labor Party's officers, August Spies, wrote, "We urgently call upon the wage-earning class to arm itself in order to be able to put forth against their exploiters such an argument which alone can be effective: *VIOLENCE!*"

Violence happened! In 1886 police attacked strikers at the McCormick Harvester Machine Company in Chicago. Afterward, Spies called for a protest meeting at a city crossing called Haymarket Square. Only a small crowd came to hear the speakers. Then around ten o'clock that night, as the last speaker was finishing, 180 policemen arrived and ordered the crowd to leave. Minutes later a bomb exploded, killing seven policemen and wounding seventy others.

According to historian Philip S. Foner, "A reign of terror swept over Chicago. The press and pulpit [church leaders] called for revenge, insisting that the bomb

This contemporary illustration of the Haymarket riot shows a bomb exploding among the police. It is based on a photograph of the event.

was the work of socialists, anarchists, and communists." Thirty-one of the protesters were charged with murder, although only eight went to trial. No one could prove who had actually thrown the bomb. All the same, one of the eight men was sentenced to fifteen years in prison, two were given life sentences, and one killed himself by exploding a bomb in his mouth. Four were hanged, including August Spies. Some called them the Haymarket martyrs.

Sixty years after the Haymarket bombing, the *Chicago Daily News* published an editorial about the incident. "The seven policemen were killed by a bomb. The identity of the bomb-thrower was never established, yet this minor flaw didn't prevent Chicago from using the "riot" to do itself great discredit. After a general panic, in which a police captain manufactured evidence, eight persons were put on trial, and . . . Four men were hanged, not so much for what they did or didn't do as for their offbeat views."

# CHAPTER FOUR

# BREAKING HEADS AND HEARTS

**A**ndrew Carnegie is remembered as a humane millionaire who donated funds to build almost three thousand libraries in cities all across the United States. Carnegie once said, "Surplus wealth is a sacred trust which its possessor is bound to administer in his lifetime for the good of the community." He also said, "The man who dies rich dies disgraced."

And yet, at another time, he was quoted as saying, "One of the serious obstacles to the improvement of our race is indiscriminate [random] charity." And "while the law [of competition] may sometimes be hard for the individual, it is best for the race, because it ensures the survival of the fittest." Andrew Carnegie became the richest man in the world. But his path to wealth was ruthless.

In the late 1800s, the new Bessemer steelmaking process made the manufacture of steel more profitable. The banks of the Monongahela River in western Pennsylvania were an ideal location for steel mills because the materials for manufacture of steel could be transported by barges on the river. In the town of Braddock, Pennsylvania, Carnegie built the Edgar Thomson Steel Works for making steel rails for railroad tracks. Later, he bought the Homestead Works, a plant that also made steel rails, on the other side of the river.

Three and a half miles (5.6 km) upriver from Homestead stood the Duquesne steel mill. It was owned by the Allegheny Bessemer Steel Company. In most steel plants, ingots (blocks of steel) were cooled before being

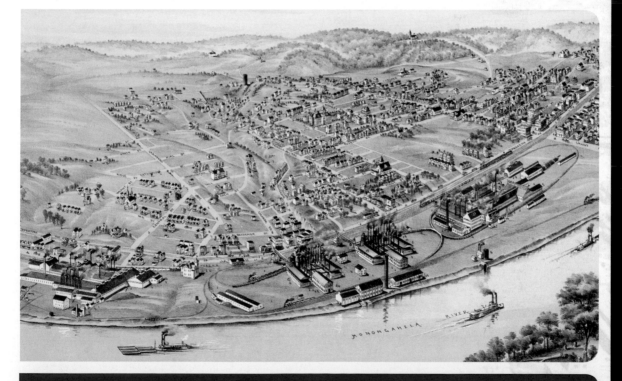

The Duquesne steel mill *(bottom center)* rivaled the production of Andrew Carnegie's Homestead Works that stood downriver.

rolled into rails. In the Duquesne mill, ingots were rolled into rails while they were still hot. This saved time and money. Since Duquesne's rails cost less, railroad builders began to buy more of them. The Homestead mill lost business.

Unhappy with his reduced profit, Carnegie started a letter-writing campaign in 1889. He sent the letters to railroad builders, telling them that Duquesne rails were inferior. The new process made them lack "homogeneity," he wrote. It was a made-up term. There was no such quality as homogeneity (uniformity) in steel, but Carnegie's tactic worked. The Duquesne steel mill received fewer orders and lost money. It sank into financial trouble. A year later, Carnegie bought the Duquesne mill. He introduced the Duquesne's rail-rolling methods into the Homestead mill as well. It was the very same process he had claimed lacked homogeneity.

Of the Homestead Works' thirty-eight hundred workers, eight hundred belonged to a union called the Amalgamated Association of Iron and Steel Workers (AA). These men were all skilled workers, mostly English, Scottish, Irish, Welsh, or German. The union didn't admit African Americans or the unskilled workers from eastern and southern Europe. They called these men Hunkies. The word was a distortion of "Hungarians" and was also applied to Czechs, Poles, Ukrainians, Slovaks, Russians, or anyone else from that area.

## THE HOMESTEAD STRIKE

Carnegie claimed to be a friend of labor. He stated that many labor-management problems were the fault of management. He left it up to Henry Clay Frick, the Carnegie Steel Company president, to enforce his stiff labor policies. On several occasions, he and Frick brought in scabs to break strikes. Scabs are workers hired to fill the jobs of striking workers.

Henry Clay Frick *(above)* was the president of the Carnegie Steel Company in the late 1800s.

The most violent confrontation happened at the Homestead Works in 1892. In June union employees asked for a wage increase. Carnegie and Frick responded by reducing wages. Carnegie told Frick to post the following message at the mill: "As the vast majority of our employees are Non-Union, the Firm has decided that the minority must give place to the majority. These works therefore will be necessarily Non-Union." Frick then announced that the mill would close on July 1 and reopen on July 6 with only nonunion labor. The AA decided to strike.

Author William Serrin, in *Homestead: The Glory and Tragedy of an American Steel Town*, writes that the union sent strikers to "the roads leading into Homestead, at the two railway stations, at the [steel] plant gates, and along both sides of the Monongahela River, to watch for attempts by the corporation to bring in strikebreakers by boat or train." By the end of June, the company had shut down six sections of the mill. Workers refused to enter any divisions of the mill that were still open.

Early on the morning of July 6, while it was still dark, two barges were towed upriver toward the Homestead Works. The barges held three hundred Pinkerton Detective Agency employees. These were not regular Pinkerton agents. Many of them were men who'd been hired off the streets—vagrants, immigrants, and the unemployed—people desperate for work. They were promised fifteen dollars a week as strikebreakers. At four in the morning, the barges were spotted by lookouts, strikers who'd been keeping watch. The lookouts

Strikers watch the river near Homestead, Pennsylvania, for strikebreakers employed by the Pinkerton Detective Agency to arrive for work at the Homestead mill.

blasted a steam whistle loudly enough to wake thousands of the town's men, women, and children. They all rushed toward the mill. Some carried rocks and sticks, but others had more threatening weapons—guns! The Pinkertons were also armed. Both sides opened fire.

The *Illustrated America* magazine reported afterward:

> NOTHING more dramatic in the History of Labor and Capital is recorded than the Incident of the 6th of July. The forces of the Nineteenth Century are Capital and Labor, united they transform the desert into a garden, in collision they convert the garden into a waste. On the 6th of July, 1892, at Homestead, Penn., the Forces met. The sound of the shock echoed through the labor markets of the world.

Townspeople sat on walls for hours, watching the battle between Pinkerton agents and the strikers as if it were a sports event. Shots rang out on both sides, and men fell wounded—or dead. Three Pinkertons and seven striking workers died. Cheers went up when, at four in the afternoon, the Pinkertons raised a white flag, admitting defeat. The strikers lowered gangplanks so the Pinkertons could move off the barges onto the riverbank. The Pinkerton's hired men were too frightened to leave the barges. They remained cowering inside them. Workers then stormed onto the barges to drag off the strikebreakers. They forced them to stumble up the riverbank between two columns of strikers, wives, and children, who screamed at them and beat them. One Pinkerton scab said, "We were clubbed at every step. Sticks, stones, and dirt were thrown at us. The women pulled us down, spat in our faces, kicked us, and tore our clothing off while the crowd jeered and cheered."

The strikebreakers were herded into the town's opera house. At eleven that night, they were taken by train to Pittsburgh, Pennsylvania. There, twenty of them were admitted to hospitals, while the others were run out of town.

Armed with rifles, the union men took possession of the Homestead Works. On the following Sunday, Pennsylvania's governor sent out eight

The state militia enters Homestead, Pennsylvania, under the order of the governor during the steel strike in 1892.

thousand members of the state militia. After the soldiers reached Homestead, four thousand of them climbed a hill above the steelworks and raised their guns. Another four thousand had landed on the other side of the Monongahela River, where they took aim at the strikers. Soon new strikebreakers, hired by Frick, entered the mill. They felt safer knowing they would be protected by the Pennsylvania militia, which had stayed in town to keep control. Within a month, some parts of the mill were operating again with scab labor.

Homestead bosses told the striking union workers that if they gave up union membership, they could apply to get their old jobs back. With no money coming in, workers' families couldn't buy food or pay the rent they owed on their company-owned houses. A few at a time, most of the union men gave in and went back to work. But not all of them did.

Some of the holdouts were blacklisted by the company. That meant they could never go back to work at the Homestead mill. A blacklisted worker couldn't get a job at any of the company's plants, anywhere. On November 20, union members voted to go back to work.

## THE FAILED ASSASSIN

On July 23, 1892, a twenty-two-year-old Russian anarchist named Alexander Berkman entered Henry Clay Frick's office building in Pittsburgh. He pretended to be an employment agent for the Homestead strikebreakers. Berkman shot Frick twice in the neck and then grabbed a knife and stabbed him in the leg. Frick not only survived, he wrestled Berkman to the floor. With the help of others, Frick pinned down the man's arms. He yelled for a deputy to force open Berkman's mouth, where they discovered what Frick had suspected. Berkman was trying to bite into a capsule of fulminate of mercury, an explosive device that could trigger a bigger bomb hidden on Berkman's body. The bomb would have blown everyone to bits. It was similar to the device one of the Haymarket prisoners had used to kill himself. When a deputy sheriff raised his gun to shoot Berkman, Frick stopped him, sparing Berkman's life. "I do not think I will die," Frick said, "but whether I do or not, the Company will pursue the same policy, and it will win."

After the attack, Alexander Berkman was sent to prison for fourteen years. Emma Goldman, a famous radical and anarchist who loved Berkman, said, "As an anarchist, I am opposed to violence. But if the people want to do away with assassins, they must do away with the conditions which produce murderers." Goldman remained faithful to Berkman until he shot himself four decades later in 1936.

Alexander Berkman *(pictured above in 1892)* was twenty-two when he tried to assassinate Carnegie Steel Company president Henry Clay Frick.

## THE PULLMAN STRIKE

In the 1890s, a massive economic depression hit worldwide. In some cities in the United States, 20 percent or more of the nation's industrial workers were out of jobs. One-quarter of the nation's railroads went bankrupt.

Located near Chicago, the Pullman Palace Car Company manufactured luxurious railroad cars. During the depression of the 1890s, however, the market for anything luxurious declined. So when the Pullman Company lost money, it laid off workers and ordered wages cut by 28 percent. At the same time, it refused to reduce the rents on company-owned houses. Eugene V. Debs, a former locomotive fireman who had become president of the American Railway Union, called a wildcat strike. (A wildcat strike is a strike that isn't approved by the union or that breaks union management rules.) Union members refused to run trains that contained Pullman cars. The strike was joined by other union railroad workers throughout the country. The Illinois governor sympathized with the strikers. He refused to call out the state militia against them. But a federal court ordered the union back to work. It noted that the unions were illegally restraining trade by keeping the railroads from running.

Eugene V. Debs *(above, in the early 1900s)* led the American Railway Union to strike in 1894. The resulting strike was put down by U.S. Army troops.

When the strikers refused to go back to work, President Grover Cleveland sent U. S. Army troops to confront them. He justified this by noting that the railroad strike disrupted mail delivery. According to historian Dick Meister, "The worst of many incidents broke out in Chicago when soldiers fired into a crowd of some 10,000 people who, spurred on by agents . . . from the railroads, had gathered to set fire to boxcars and

Strikers attempt to move an engine and car during the Pullman Strike in 1894. This illustration of the strike comes from a periodical printed that same year.

otherwise violently protest the movement of trains by the army. Twenty-five people were killed, 60 badly injured." The strike failed.

Debs was jailed along with other union officers. During his time in jail, Debs became a Socialist. He noted, "The capitalists own the tools they do not use, and the workers use the tools they do not own."

## HEART OF THE AWL

In Coeur d'Alene, in northern Idaho, federal troops had been called out when silver miners struck violently in 1892. (*Coeur d'Alene* is French for "heart of the awl." An awl is a pointed tool used to pierce leather.) Silver mining was difficult and dangerous work. Miners worked for ten-hour shifts. They were each given only three ordinary candles to light the underground tunnels where they worked. Cave-ins, explosions, and other accidents happened frequently. Yet mineowners in the Coeur d'Alene mining area considered these calamities part of the cost of doing business.

Mineowners around Coeur d'Alene had slashed miners' wages by 15 percent in 1892. When the miners struck in protest, the owners hired strikebreakers. Once again, the Pinkertons came in to infiltrate the union and report to the owners what the strikers were planning. The situation became explosive, literally, when the union discovered these spies in their midst. Angry miners used dynamite to blow up a four-story mill at a mine. The Idaho governor called in federal troops. They arrested six hundred miners and locked them up behind 14-foot-high (4 m) fences for two months without arrest warrants, charges, or trials required by the U.S. Constitution. Later, the miners were finally released.

Silver miners in the Coeur d'Alene region remained dissatisfied and angry. A few years afterward, in April 1899, officials of the Western Federation of Miners demanded that the Coeur d'Alene Bunker Hill Mine recognize their union. The mineowners' response was to fire all union members. Union men responded by planting sixty boxes of dynamite beneath the Bunker Hill Mine's concentrator. This large, expensive piece of equipment separated silver ore from sand and rocks. The explosion was heard 20 miles (32 km) away. In May Idaho governor Frank Steunenberg requested federal troops. The troops arrested every male—miners, bartenders, a doctor, a preacher, a postmaster, a school superintendent, and even the sheriff—in the union-controlled town of Burke, Idaho. The federal troops herded the men into boxcars and then held them captive in an old barn for several months, while their families tried to survive without any income. Governor Steunenberg believed he had destroyed the Western Federation of Miners.

But the union did not die. Steunenberg did. As he opened his back gate to walk through it on New Year's Eve six years later, a piece of fishing line attached to the gate pulled a blasting cap to set off a bomb at the gate's bottom. The resulting explosion blew Steunenberg 10 feet (3 m) into the air. Authorities believed the murder was a revenge killing plotted by the Western Federation of Miners.

William "Big Bill" Haywood *(above)* headed the Western Federation of Miners. He was often photographed in profile because his right eye had been blinded in childhood.

Once again, the Pinkerton Detective Agency entered the picture. Its most famous agent, James McParland, who had earlier infiltrated the Molly Maguires, went to Denver, Colorado. There, with the help of Colorado officials, the Pinkertons kidnapped William "Big Bill" Haywood, the head of the Western Federation of Miners. They kept him imprisoned inside a special train that traveled nonstop to Boise, Idaho. In Boise, Haywood went on trial in 1907 for supposedly masterminding the murder of Frank Steunenberg.

## THE TRIAL OF THE CENTURY

Even when it first began, the Haywood court case was named the "trial of the century." What made the trial so famous was the cast of characters: Big Bill Haywood; his famous defense lawyer, Clarence Darrow; and prosecutor William Borah, well-known in Idaho. Borah went on to become an Idaho state senator and a close ally of Theodore Roosevelt, who was president of the United States at the time of the trial. Clarence Darrow later won fame as the defense lawyer in the Scopes Trial, or Monkey Trial. (In that trial, he defended a teacher in Tennessee who taught the then controversial scientific theory of evolution.)

The Haywood jury consisted of twelve bewhiskered Idaho farmers, all of them expected to be hostile to labor unions. But as defense counsel

The chief prosecution witness *(on left, facing right)* testifies against Big Bill Haywood *(third from right)* during Haywood's trial. Defense lawyer Clarence Darrow is seated sixth from the right.

Clarence Darrow made his pleas, the jurors listened closely. Gasps of astonishment filled the courthouse, when after a two-and-a-half-month trial, Bill Haywood was declared not guilty. Afterward, he became president of the newly formed IWW, the Industrial Workers of the World.

President Theodore Roosevelt had referred to Bill Haywood and his allies as "undesirable citizens." At the end of the trial, Emma Goldman telegraphed President Roosevelt, "Undesirable citizens victorious! Rejoice!"

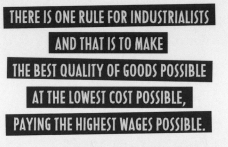

# CHAPTER FIVE

## IWW VERSUS AFL

Industrial Workers of the World called themselves by another name too—the Wobblies. Historians aren't exactly sure of the origins of the name, but it's believed that the name Wobbly started with a Chinese restaurant owner. He was a union sympathizer who couldn't quite pronounce the letters IWW. Members grew to like the name Wobbly.

According to Big Bill Haywood, the IWW union was "big enough to take in the black man, the white man; big enough to take in all nationalities—an organization that will be strong enough to obliterate [wipe out] state boundaries, to obliterate national boundaries." He wanted the IWW to become "One Big Union." It would welcome trade union workers, industrial union workers, Socialists, anarchists, women, people of color, immigrants, and unskilled workers, alike. One Big Union was part of Haywood's dream for a socialistic society.

But it wasn't everyone's. One of the most influential American unions at the beginning of the twentieth century was the American Federation of Labor (AFL). It had begun in 1886 as a collection of trade unions under the leadership of Samuel Gompers, a cigar maker. Gompers was born in London and immigrated to New York, where he joined a union. Gompers's first AFL office was a small room in a shed. His son was the office boy. The union's treasury held only $160. As Gompers said, his position meant "much work, little pay, and very little honor."

His union grew quickly. By 1890 the American Federation of Labor represented 250,000 workers. In two more years, the AFL had grown to more than one million members, representing mostly skilled workers in various trades such as carpenters, printers, and brick masons. Trade unions were usually limited to members trained or experienced in that one particular kind of work. Gompers said, "The trade union movement represents the organized economic power of the workers. It is in reality the most potent and the most direct social insurance the workers can establish." He believed that workers should not only have the right to earn a living. They should also play a meaningful role as citizens in the American political process by informing themselves about important issues. His definition of citizens, though, was narrow, excluding women, the foreign born, and unskilled workers.

Samuel Gompers *(above)* served as president of the American Federation of Labor for forty years, beginning in 1886.

Gompers opposed the idea of one big union, the goal Bill Haywood hoped for. He wanted the AFL to coordinate the goals of the separate unions within each trade. He favored collective bargaining with employers, negotiating directly with the employer to try to reach agreements. Gompers also believed that labor and politicians could work together on legal issues that would affect jobs, rather than staging confrontations with industry management.

The IWW, on the other hand, wanted to bring skilled and unskilled workers of all classes and colors into one union. It claimed that the AFL should be changed to "ASL" for "American *Separation* of Labor." The difference in the ideals of the two organizations—the big, strong AFL and the smaller, less powerful IWW—became obvious during a huge strike in the Lawrence, Massachusetts, textile mills in 1912.

## THE LAWRENCE STRIKE

Most of the textile workers in the Northeast at this time were recent immigrants. They came from Italy, Poland, Germany, Lithuania, Syria, and twenty other countries. Most of them, because they spoke little English, lived in poor neighborhoods filled with immigrants from the same country. Conditions were harsh, and the rooms they lived in were small and crowded. This close contact spread illness among workers already weakened by miserable factory conditions. In the factories, dampness and poor ventilation let wool and cotton particles float through the air into the workers' lungs. Half of the women who worked as spinners in the textile mills died before the age of twenty-five from illness or because of accidents caused by fatigue.

Of the approximately forty thousand textile mill workers in Lawrence in 1912, only twenty-five hundred belonged to the local AFL. This was not surprising, since the AFL didn't recruit women or foreign-born, unskilled workers. Surprisingly, the more radical and inclusive IWW had even fewer members in Lawrence. Only three hundred IWW members had paid their dues. Several hundred others hadn't.

In January 1912, the state of Massachusetts passed a law reducing the workweek from fifty-six to fifty-four hours. Because of the two-hour time cut, millowners demanded that workers speed up production to keep up profits. But at the same time, they cut two hours of pay from the weekly wages of each worker. Workers who had averaged only $8.76 per week weren't willing to lose thirty-one cents. It could have bought three loaves of bread. The workers rebelled. The strike that followed is often called the Strike for Three Loaves.

Long before, in 1619 at Jamestown, Polish men had begun the first known strike in what became the United States. Almost three hundred years later, in Lawrence, Polish women were the first to shut down their looms and march through the streets, shouting, "*Nie dosc zold*. Short pay! Short pay!"

Italian workers followed. At one mill, the Italians took more dramatic action. They ran through the aisles cutting power to the spinning machines and slicing cloth being woven on the looms. Thousands of other workers joined the crowd. The striking workers held a mass meeting at the city's Franco-Belgian Hall. They telegraphed IWW leader Joseph Ettor to come to Lawrence. Ettor, twenty-seven, could speak English, Italian, and Polish, and he understood Hungarian and Yiddish as well. He came to Lawrence to help the strikers form a strike committee to set forth the workers' demands.

## CALL OUT THE MILITIA!

In response to the Lawrence Strike, the governor of Massachusetts called out the state militia and the state police. *Outlook Magazine* carried the following account from one member of the militia: "Our company of militia went down to Lawrence during the first days of the strike. Most of them had to leave Harvard [College] to do it, but they rather enjoyed going down there to have a fling at those people." In the freezing weather, the strikebreakers stood on roofs and used hoses to drench the crowds of striking workers.

Crowds of strikers face off against the militia in Lawrence, Massachusetts, in January 1912. The strike of textile workers, led by the IWW, included men and women of many different nationalities.

Joseph Ettor was arrested and imprisoned on a trumped-up charge of murdering one of the strikers, although he'd been 3 miles (5 km) from the scene. The IWW sent Bill Haywood to Lawrence to replace him, along with union activist Elizabeth Gurley Flynn. Haywood advised the strikers to practice passive resistance (nonviolent methods), instead of violence. He declared later that he realized "labor wars of the old type are passing. I should never think of conducting a strike in the old way. There will never be another Coeur d'Alene. . . . I, for one, have turned my back on violence. It wins nothing. When we strike now, we strike with our hands in our pockets. We have a new kind of violence—the havoc we raise with money by laying down our tools. Our strength lies in the overwhelming power of numbers."

For Bill Haywood to preach nonviolence was certainly something new. And in another tactic of the Socialist-leaning IWW, Elizabeth Gurley Flynn took charge of a new and daring plan. The union would evacuate the strikers' children and temporarily place them with caring families in other cities. This way the striking women would not have to worry about caring for and feeding their children while they were on strike and receiving no pay. The first group of 120 children was loaded onto a train bound for New York City. They were met by a huge crowd of Italian Socialists singing the international workers' anthem, the "Internationale."

Children of strikers arrive in New York during the Lawrence Strike in 1912.

So comrades, come rally;

And the last fight let us face;

The *Internationale* unites the human race.

Two weeks later, another ninety-two children from striking families arrived in New York City, where they marched down Fifth Avenue waving banners. Afterward, they were taken to volunteers' homes to be fed and cared for.

IWW members march through New York City in 1912 with the children of Lawrence strikers.

On February 24, an additional group of children was to be sent by train, this time to Philadelphia. Later, a member of the Philadelphia Women's Committee who had gone to Lawrence to accompany them testified under oath. She described the scene.

> When the time came to depart, the children, arranged in a long line, two by two in an orderly procession with the parents near at hand, were about to make their way to the train when the police . . . closed in on us with their clubs, beating right and left with no thought of the children who then were in desperate danger of being trampled to death. The mothers and the children were thus hurled in a mass, and bodily dragged to a military truck and even then clubbed, irrespective of the cries of the panic-stricken mothers and children. We can scarcely find words with which to describe this display of brutality.

## BREAD AND ROSES

The attack on the children proved to be a huge tactical mistake on the part of the factory owners and authorities. Newspaper headlines blazed with accounts of police brutally beating children, as in the *New York Times* banner: HEADS BROKEN OVER AN ORDER TO PREVENT STRIKERS SHIPPING THEIR CHILDREN AWAY. People throughout the United States were appalled. The U.S. Senate held hearings where strikers told their stories. The millowners defended their policies. But public sympathy was with the strikers and their families.

In Lawrence, after attending mass meetings during the strike, workers would often pour into the streets shouting and singing. Singing seemed to raise the spirits and renew the determination of striking men and women. Elizabeth Gurley Flynn declared, "The women worked in the mills for lower pay and in addition had all the housework and care of the children. There was considerable male opposition to women going to meetings and marching on the picket line. We resolutely set out to combat these notions. The women wanted to picket!"

During a parade through Lawrence, a group of women workers carried banners that read "Bread and Roses," meaning they needed beauty in their lives as well as food for their families. The phrase became a poem that was set to music and sung with fervor by laborers across the United States:

As we come marching, marching in the beauty of the day,
A million darkened kitchens, a thousand mill lofts gray,
Are touched with all the radiance that a sudden sun discloses,
For the people hear us singing: "Bread and roses! Bread and roses!"

As we come marching, marching, unnumbered women dead
Go crying through our singing their ancient cry for bread.
Small art and love and beauty their drudging spirits knew.
Yes, it is bread we fight for—but we fight for roses, too!

The growing determination of the women united the Lawrence strikers. Bill Haywood exclaimed later, "It was a wonderful strike, the most significant strike, the greatest strike that has ever been carried on in this country or any other country. And the most significant part of that strike was that it was a democracy. The strikers had a committee of 56, representing 27 different languages. . . . And immediately behind that committee was a substitute committee of another 56 prepared in the event of the original committee's being arrested [and] thrown in jail."

Not all unionists supported Big Bill Haywood and the IWW. John Golden, the president of the United Textile Workers of America (part of the AFL), tried to prevent his union of skilled workers from joining the Lawrence walkout. Golden blamed the IWW for conducting a violence-prone strike. Arriving in Lawrence, Golden managed to persuade the millowners to offer his trade union workers a 5 percent pay increase. His union accepted, and those members returned to their jobs.

But not the Wobblies! They refused the 5 percent raise and kept on striking. By the middle of March, the millowners decided that the strike had to end soon because the mills were losing too much money. They offered a general 7 percent increase, not just for the workers of Lawrence but for all the 250,000 workers in the cotton and woolen mills of northern New England. It wasn't as much as the IWW had asked for, but it came at the right time. The mills had been almost completely shut down by the strike for two months. The hungry, destitute, and desperate workers were beginning to straggle back to their old jobs without the blessing of the unions. When the IWW negotiated an average 7½ percent increase in pay, the remaining strikers rushed back triumphantly to the looms and spindles they had deserted in January.

Haywood was a hero. But that wouldn't last long.

## SHIFTING OPINION

The American people were becoming more and more dismayed by the violence of both unions and management. Even though workers were often guilty of aggression during strikes, the public's sympathy was shifting to favor them. In 1911 the Triangle Shirtwaist Company fire in a New York City garment factory aroused sympathy and outrage. After fire broke out on the tenth floor of the shirtwaist factory, workers discovered that the fire doors were locked. They had no way to flee. One survivor, a man, recalled, "There were flames all around in no time. Three girls, I think from the floor below, came rushing past me. Their clothes were on fire. I grabbed the fire pails and tried to pour the water on them, but they did not stop. They ran screaming toward the windows." A total of 148 workers died from plunging out of high windows, from flames, or from asphyxiation. The dead were mainly immigrant girls between sixteen and twenty-three years old. According to the *New York Times*, "Most of them could barely speak English. Almost all were the main support of their hard-working families. . . . [Fire] Chief Crocker said it was an outrage. He spoke bitterly of the way in which the Manufacturers' Association [a management group] had called a meeting in Wall Street [New York's economic center] *against* [Crocker's] proposal for enforcing better methods of protection for employees in cases of fire." Very

This Brooklyn, New York, newspaper shows the outrage of the public following a deadly fire at the Triangle Shirtwaist Company in 1911.

slowly, owners were beginning to get the message that this kind of publicity about their poor treatment of workers was bad for business.

## WORKERS ARE CUSTOMERS

About the same time, one leading businessman, Henry Ford, found a way he could produce automobiles—the era's newest invention—more cheaply. He figured out how to streamline his manufacturing methods

SWEAT AND BLOOD

and thereby cut costs. Ford divided the manufacturing process for his automobile into eighty-four different steps. Individual workers were trained
to perform just one of the steps as cars rolled along an assembly line. The
first of these assembly-line Model T Fords rolled out of the Ford factory
in Detroit, Michigan, in 1913. By paying his employees a little more, Ford
saw that he might be able to turn his workers into his customers. A year

later, Ford raised his
workers' pay to five
dollars a day. He was
right. His workers be-
gan to buy Model Ts.

Finished Model T Fords come out of the factory ready for delivery in the
1910s. Henry Ford paid his employees wages that were high enough to allow
employees to buy the product they made, the Model T.

> I AM NOT UNAWARE THAT [OUR] LEADERS BETRAY,
> AND SELL OUT, AND PLAY FALSE.
> BUT THIS KNOWLEDGE DOES NOT OUTWEIGH THE FACT THAT . . .
> THE WORKING CLASS, IS EXPLOITED, DRIVEN,
> FOUGHT BACK WITH THE WEAPON OF STARVATION,
> WITH GUNS AND WITH VENAL COURTS
> WHENEVER THEY STRIKE
> FOR CONDITIONS MORE HUMAN, MORE CIVILIZED.

—LABOR ORGANIZER MOTHER JONES (MARY HARRIS JONES), 1925

# CHAPTER SIX

# THE MOST HATED MAN IN THE UNITED STATES

In 1913 another brutal labor fight was brewing in the West, in the Colorado coalfields. The coal companies there owned the houses the workers lived in and controlled much of their lives. According to Samuel Gompers, "It was a common saying that children [of miners] were brought into the world by the company doctor, lived in a company house or hut, were nurtured by the company store, baptized by the company parson [preacher], buried in a company coffin, and laid away in a company graveyard." A miner's pay averaged about $3.50 per day, which in another setting should have been just barely enough to cover rent and other necessities. But miners were paid in script—shortened to scrip. These coupons could be spent only in stores owned by each of the mining companies, where prices were high. Scrip paid for food, clothes, shoes, the dynamite used for blasting coal, crowbars, and any other tools the miners needed and had to pay for. If they ran out of scrip, as they often did, the company store allowed them to charge what they bought. But this system kept miners in debt to the coal companies. In the words of a popular song:

> You load sixteen tons, what do you get?
> Another day older and deeper in debt.
> Saint Peter don't you call me 'cause I can't go,
> I owe my soul to the company store.

Coal was the main source of fuel energy for homes and factories at this time, but working in the mines was exceedingly dangerous. Between 1884 and 1912, a total of 42,898 coal miners died in mining accidents in the United States. As was true in the New England textile mills, most of the Colorado miners were recent immigrants. They spoke twenty-four different languages and lived barely above poverty level. By contrast, the largest of the Colorado coal companies, the Colorado Fuel and Iron, was owned by one of the two richest men in the United States, John D. Rockefeller. (The other was Andrew Carnegie.)

The miners' union, the United Mine Workers of America (UMWA), held a meeting in the southern Colorado town of Trinidad in 1913. At the meeting, Colorado miners spoke about their hazardous working conditions and the unfair company rules they had to live by. Members of the UMWA then called a strike. They demanded the mining companies recognize the

John D. Rockefeller *(pictured above in 1913)* was a cofounder of Standard Oil and president of the company from 1870 to 1897. He also owned Colorado Fuel and Iron, the largest coal company in Colorado.

Mary Harris Jones, known as Mother Jones, wrote about the struggles of the miners in Colorado.

union, a 10 percent increase in wages, and an eight-hour workday. They also wanted the right to shop in any store and to rent whichever houses they wanted to live in. Not surprisingly, the coal companies rejected all these demands.

A famous labor organizer traveled to Colorado to support the strikers. Mary Harris Jones, affectionately known as Mother Jones, became a widow when her husband and four children died in a yellow fever epidemic. She moved to Chicago, where she became a dressmaker, but her home and shop were destroyed in the Great Chicago Fire of 1871. Unbowed by misfortune, Mother Jones, white-haired and in her fifties, became active in the unions, especially the United Mine Workers of America.

After the Colorado miners walked out, Mother Jones wrote about the ways Colorado Fuel and Iron used scab workers to keep the mines running. "The operators were bringing in Mexicans to work as scabs in the mines. In this operation they were protected by the military all the way from the Mexican borders. They were brought in to the strike territory without knowing the conditions, promised enormous wages and easy work. They were packed in cattle cars, in charge of company gunmen, and if when arriving, they attempted to leave, they were shot. Hundreds of these poor fellows had been lured into the mines with promises of free land. When they got off the trains, they were driven like cattle into the mines by gunmen."

American author Jack London, a Socialist and author of *The Call of the Wild* (1903), is quoted as saying about scabs, "After God had finished the rattlesnake, the toad, and the vampire, he had some awful substance left with which he made a scab. A scab is a two-legged animal with a corkscrew soul, a water brain, a combination backbone of jelly and glue. Where others have hearts he carries a tumor of rotten principles."

Although scabs were hated by the striking workers, most of the scabs were poor men trying to earn a wage any way they could.

## THE TENT COLONIES

The mining companies forced the families of the striking miners to leave their company-owned houses. To shelter them, UMWA members put up tent cities at several locations. However, the tents provided little protection from Colorado's cold, wet weather.

The largest strikers' tent colony housed about twelve hundred miners and their families. It was located in Ludlow, Colorado. During the strike, the coal companies hired guards and ruffians to harass the strikers with the "Death Special." This was an armored car that held a mounted machine

Striking miners and their families moved to tent cities, such as the one in Ludlow, Colorado *(above)*, after being forced out of their company-owned homes.

gun that the hired guards fired at the tent cities. In the Forbes, Colorado, tent colony, 148 bullets shredded a single tent. In that tent, one miner was killed and a boy was shot nine times in his leg. The angry strikers fought back with guns. As a result of the violence, the mineowners requested aid from the Colorado state militia.

In 1913 Mother Jones was arrested for organizing mine workers, which was an illegal in Colorado at that time. When she was released, she traveled the country giving speeches about conditions at the Colorado mines and urging a congressional investigation. When she returned to Colorado in January 1914, she was arrested again. More than one thousand women and children gathered at the militia offices in support of her. The militia's cavalry, bayonets drawn, spurred their horses toward the women to scatter them, injuring a number of the women. Mother Jones was later released.

On Easter Sunday 1914, the hired guards began to machine-gun the tent city at Ludlow. Expecting this kind of attack, several of the tent occupants had earlier dug pits beneath wooden tent floors to hide in for safety. Many women and children took refuge in the pits. On this day, the guards also threw kerosene onto the tents and set fire to them. The next day, two women and ten children were found suffocated to death in a pit beneath one of the burned tents. Eight other people had been shot, including a child.

Women and children march on the streets of Trinidad, Colorado, in support of Mother Jones.

The fire in Ludlow destroyed the entire tent colony, killing twelve people who were hiding from the militia in pits beneath their tents.

A report published by the Colorado Bar Association states, "What actually happened in the days that led up to the [Ludlow] Massacre is known only by those now dead. What we read in accounts, narratives, and histories has been influenced as much by the bias and prejudice of the writers as by the preconceived attitudes of the day about Capital [Business] and Labor. The principal players have been shown as both noble and sinister. Coal operators were heartless profiteers, mine guards thugs, militiamen trigger-happy goons, union leaders self-serving opportunists and miners hot-tempered foreigners. What is clear is that the miners, as a group, were constantly bullied by the militiamen."

Public outrage flared after the Ludlow Massacre but so did the battle between miners and strikebreakers. The Colorado governor asked President Woodrow Wilson to intervene. The president sent in U.S. Army troops, who were more restrained in their tactics than the state militia had been. Wilson couldn't convince the coal companies and the strikers to come to a settlement. Finally, just two weeks before Christmas 1914, the UMWA gave up because union funds, which paid for the striking miners' relief, were used up.

## IMAGE CONTROL

For decades newspaper cartoons had portrayed capitalists as richly dressed, overfed bullies. They had shown workers as determined muscular men in shirtsleeves. In the second decade of the 1900s, new technology allowed newspapers to publish photographs. The photos showed militia attacking workers, workers' families looking underfed and pathetic, and tent cities covered with snow. Labor organizations had already learned how to use these photos and newspaper stories to arouse public sympathy. Gradually capitalists began to mount a public-relations counterattack.

For example, after the brutal Colorado miners' strike, mineowner John D. Rockefeller became known as "the most hated man in America." This was somewhat unfair since Rockefeller had contributed a good part of his fortune to charity. But the title had an unexpected effect on the man and, eventually, on all of the corporate United States. Rockefeller decided it was time to improve his image. In September 1915, he sent his son John D. Rockefeller Jr. from New York to Colorado to speak to a gathering of miners. Although his father's company had made no concessions to the workers, John D. Jr. told them, "We are all partners in a way. Capital [business] can't get along without you men, and you men can't get along without capital. When anybody comes along and tells you that capital and labor can't get along together, that man is your worst enemy. We are getting along friendly enough here in this mine right now, and there is no reason why you men cannot get along with the managers of my company when I am back in New York."

Was this talk successful? Mother Jones commented later, "John Rockefeller [Jr.] is a nice young man but . . . we went away feeling that he could not possibly understand the aspirations [hopes] of the working class. He was as alien as is one species from another; as alien as is stone from wheat."

Undeterred, Rockefeller Sr. hired a public relations man named Ivy Lee. Lee supposedly came up with the idea that Rockefeller Sr. should carry a roll of dimes with him. He would give them, one at a time, to any children he might meet. In a more serious maneuver, Lee started to publish misleading information about the Colorado strike. The information claimed that the Ludlow miners themselves had set the fires that destroyed the tent colony and cost innocent lives. Lee's methods were unethical. But that capitalists were starting to care what the public thought about them was a new and surprising turn of events.

## BULLETS, BOOTS, AND BALANCE SHEETS

World War I (1914–1918) began in Europe in the summer of 1914. During this conflict, France, Great Britain, and its allies (together known as the Allies) were pitted in battle against Germany and its supporters, Austria and Turkey (the Central powers). German submarines targeted and blew up Allied ships crossing the Atlantic. As a result, travel and commercial shipping across the ocean became very dangerous. The flow of European immigrant labor and goods into the United States slowed dramatically during the war years.

The United States did not immediately join the Allies in the war. But during the early years of the conflict, U.S. factories went into high gear to produce bullets, boots, helmets, railroad cars, ships, and other war materials for the Allies. Selling these supplies to the Allied nations in Europe was extremely profitable. U.S. exports increased from $825 million in 1914 to $3.2 billion in 1916.

**Success**
*in* **War —**

depends on co-operation and good feeling between the captains and privates in our volunteer, wage-paid American industrial army now stationed at—

**Fort Factory**

This World War I poster encourages workers not to strike at factories during the war.

When the United States finally entered the war in the spring of 1917, two million America men were quickly called to serve in the military. This was the first time that the United States had required adult men to register for a military draft since the Civil War. The draft dramatically cut into the number of men available to work in factories, just when the factories were producing at peak volume and needed large numbers of workers. African Americans from the rural South surged north to industrial cities such as Pittsburgh, Pennsylvania; Chicago, Illinois; and Detroit, Michigan, to fill this need. A 2002 PBS documentary, *A History of Us*, points out, "Entire communities pulled up roots and headed north. Although African Americans faced segregation and racism in overcrowded northern cities, many still believed the North offered greater opportunities for themselves and their children."

Whether they thought of it as an opportunity or a duty, American women also flocked to northern factories for jobs. Many joined a support group called the National Women's Trade Union League of America. They asked for an eight-hour workday and equal pay for equal work. (At that time, men's wages were at least twice as high as wages for women.) They got neither.

## LABOR AND THE WAR

Different labor organizations had differing reactions to the war. After the United States entered the conflict, the American Federation of Labor promised that its members would not strike for the duration of the war. This patriotic promise won new friends for the AFL, and membership increased almost 50 percent during the war years to 3.2 million.

The IWW and other Socialist groups, however, loudly opposed the war and the draft. For this reason, support for these groups shrank and attitudes toward the IWW became especially bitter. Many Socialists evaded the draft by escaping to Mexico, which did not participate in the war. Socialist speakers in the United States cried out from street corners: "Why should American workers kill German workers to enrich the capitalists of each country?" they asked. The Wobblies and other unions struck against the lumber industry, shipping companies, and other industries that manufactured vital war supplies. These strikes made unions even less popular with the public. Then the U.S. government took action against them.

In September 1917, Federal Bureau of Investigation (FBI) agents raided forty-eight IWW meeting halls across the United States. In all, 165 IWW leaders were arrested for conspiring to hinder the draft, for encouraging desertion from the army, and for sabotage. On trial in Chicago, nearly one hundred Wobblies, including Bill Haywood, were found guilty. They were sentenced to federal prison terms of from ten to twenty years and fined from ten thousand to twenty thousand dollars.

Any public support for the IWW was further weakened two months later. In November 1917, the Communist Bolshevik Party, led by Vladimir Lenin, overthrew the czar's government in Russia. Fear of Communist and other left-leaning groups in the United States increased. In fact, the Sedition Act of 1918 took aim at all of them: anarchists, Socialists, pacifists, and even at certain labor leaders. The law read in part, "Whoever, when the United States is at war, shall willfully . . . utter, print, write, or publish any disloyal, profane, scurrilous [vulgar], or abusive language about the form of government of the United States, or the Constitution of the United States, or the military or naval forces of the United States . . . or shall willfully urge, incite, or advocate any curtailment [lessening] of production . . . or by word or act oppose the cause of the United States therein, shall be punished by a fine of not more than $10,000 or imprisonment for not more than 20 years, or both."

The law definitely applied to Russian-born Emma Goldman, the ardent anarchist, who believed the war was a rich man's war. She encouraged men to refuse to be drafted. For that she was convicted and sent to prison. Later, the U.S. Congress passed the Anti-Anarchist Act, allowing the government to deport aliens (foreigners) living in the United States. On December 21, 1919, Emma Goldman and her lover, the would-be assassin Alexander Berkman, and 247 other foreign-born radicals and political extremists were herded aboard the ship USS *Buford* at dawn and deported, first to Finland and then to Russia.

Also arrested, accused, and found guilty under the Espionage Act, which made it a crime to pass along military information, was labor leader and Socialist Party member Eugene Debs. He was sentenced to ten years in prison. Bill Haywood received a sentence of twenty years in prison. Both the Espionage Act and the Sedition Act were eventually repealed, but Bill Haywood didn't wait around for that to happen. Out on bail while his case was being appealed to the U.S. Supreme Court, Big Bill jumped bail. He obtained passage on a ship that sailed for Sweden. From there he entered Russia. A news story reported shortly afterward that William Haywood "has joined the Communist Party and has definitely severed all connection with the IWW."

Still a believer in unions, Haywood became a delegate to the first Congress of the Red Trade Union International. This meeting in Moscow, Russia, brought together Communists from many countries, including a few who had managed to arrive from the United States. The meeting stated, "Communists must explain to the proletariat [workers] that their problems can be answered . . . by revolutionizing the trade unions." Lenin couldn't attend that meeting, but he sent a message. "Communism will triumph in the trade unions," he noted. "No power on earth can avert the collapse of capitalism and the victory of the working class over the bourgeoisie."

Without Bill Haywood, U.S. Wobbly membership dwindled. Haywood remained in Russia until he died in 1928. Half his ashes are buried in the Kremlin (Russia's seat of government) near the tomb of Lenin. The other half are buried in Chicago, close to the monument to the Haymarket martyrs.

## "AMERICA IS FOR AMERICANS"

As regard for the IWW dwindled in the United States, regard for Samuel Gompers and the AFL rose. Right after Haywood fled to Russia, Gompers sent a letter to an associate at Haverford College in Pennsylvania that reflected the surge of nationalism that followed the end of the war in 1918. Stressing that a large pool of cheap immigrant labor depresses wages, Gompers wrote, "So many immigrants coming into this country [after World War I] will break down the standard of living of our people. . . . Labor does not desire to erect a wall around our country and prevent the poor of other nations from entering. It does declare that America is for Americans alone. . . . Those who favor unrestricted immigration care nothing for the people. They are simply desirous of flooding the country with unskilled as well as skilled labor of other lands for the purpose of breaking down American standards. America, however, where men are free to voice their desires for greater and still greater advancement in economic conditions, is the greatest country on earth. Its people live better than anywhere else, and the trade unions are responsible for maintaining those standards."

With his attack on immigrants, Gompers sounded like industrialists of the era. At the end of a big steelworkers strike in 1919, for example, the steel companies blamed it on "aliens" and "the un-America teachings of radical strike agitators." Gompers's view fit the postwar mood of the nation, and by the time of his death in 1924, the AFL has grown to nearly three million members.

**WE LEAVE OUR HOMES IN THE MORNING,
WE KISS OUR CHILDREN GOODBYE,
WHILE WE SLAVE FOR THE BOSSES
OUR CHILDREN SCREAM AND CRY.
BUT UNDERSTAND, ALL WORKERS,
OUR UNION THEY DO FEAR.
LET'S STAND TOGETHER, WORKERS,
AND HAVE A UNION HERE.**

—FACTORY WORKER AND UNION ORGANIZER ELLA MAE WIGGINS
(1900–1929), "MILL MOTHER'S LAMENT"

# CHAPTER SEVEN

# THE DECADE THAT ROARED

When the 1920s arrived, Americans wanted "greater advancement in economic conditions"—a bigger piece of the pie. Americans had survived a world war in which eight and a half million people had died and twenty-one million had been wounded, plus a worldwide flu epidemic that killed another fifty million people. After those horrors, Americans wanted to enjoy life. And businesses were prospering enough to give workers more benefits. In the postwar United States, employees won wage increases, shorter working hours, and paid vacations—for the first time in history. Employers provided worker cafeterias and recreation areas. The goal of this welfare capitalism was to keep workers happy so they would not join labor unions. Secretary of Labor James

John Davis said, "The long work day and the long work week is as dead as a dodo. . . . Prosperity is not the product of the classes; it is the product of the masses . . . labor-saving machines are rapidly becoming leisure-producing machines."

Calvin Coolidge, then governor of Massachusetts, said, "There has been a great economic change for the better among all wage-earners. . . . The great outstanding fact in the economic life of America is that the wealth of the Nation is owned by the people of the Nation. . . . Two persons out of three have money in the savings bank—men, women, and children. . . . Our great need now is for more of everything for everybody."

Just eight days after he spoke those words, Calvin Coolidge called out the Massachusetts National Guard to break a strike of Boston police officers. The Boston police were striking for permission to form a union. They'd also asked for higher pay and more vacation. Coolidge not only denied the police officers' demands, he hired a whole new police force and refused to let the strikers have their old jobs back. This brought Calvin Coolidge national attention. A few months later, he was elected vice president of the United States under President Warren G. Harding. When Harding died in 1923, Coolidge became president, serving until 1929.

Even with postwar prosperity, conditions remained deplorable in certain industries, especially the southern textile mills. Antiunion feelings were still strong there. In North Carolina, factory worker Ella Mae Wiggins testified, "I'm the mother of nine. Four died with the whooping cough, all at once. I was working nights, I asked the super to put me on days, so's I could tend 'em when they had their bad spells. But he wouldn't. I don't know why. So I had to quit, and then there wasn't no money for medicine, and they just died."

Becoming an ardent union supporter, Ella Mae, a white woman, helped to organize African American workers. On September 14, 1929, as she rode in a truck with other union members to attend a meeting, an armed mob turned them back. On their way home, a car blocked the road. Antiunion thugs jumped out and began shooting. Shot in the chest, Ella Mae Wiggins died. She was twenty-nine years old.

## WORKING INSIDE THE LINES

A company union is a labor union of the employees of a single firm. Company unions were more easily controlled by business owners than the old-fashioned trade unions, and workers in company unions couldn't be called on to join strikes by national unions. This new kind of unionism, which began early in the twentieth century, concerned Samuel Gompers. He worried that his AFL might attract fewer workers.

Gompers also worried about the impact on workers and on the union movement of Henry Ford's assembly-line formula for production. Each worker had only one repetitive task to perform as cars came together piece by piece. Gompers said, "Because [Ford] has taken it for granted men are satisfied if they have high wages and a short work day, he has taken away their right to participate in creative work. Because he fails to appreciate the spiritual meaning of craftsmanship, he finds no place for the trade union movement." Gompers's long AFL reign ended with his death in 1924.

## CRASH!

At the end of July 1929, *Time* magazine reported, "One of the reasons why so much money is being poured into the stock market is that there are many new stocks to buy . . . corporations are issuing stock, taking the public into partnership." An Episcopal bishop declared that playing the stock market was not gambling (a vice according to many religions) and therefore was not immoral. Americans began to believe that everybody had a right to be rich—until October 1929.

There had been warnings. As early as March 1928, Secretary of Labor James John Davis had declared there were too many workers for the available jobs. "You can make all the boots and shoes needed annually in America in about six months, and you can blow all the window glass needed in America in seventeen days. You can dig all the coal necessary in six months with the men now in the industry. Because of our increase in population in the last eight or ten years, it now should take 140 men to supply the needs of the country where 100 could do so [back then]. Instead of that, and in spite of our having 20,000,000 more people, the needs of the country are fully supplied with 7% fewer workers than we needed in 1919." Davis had already claimed that the coal industry was "overmanned" by as many as 300,000 workers. So, the mineowners could feel justified in cutting that many jobs.

Around that same time, the commissioner of the U.S. Bureau of Labor Statistics reported on the impact of mechanization in industry. "Every machine that is built to do the work of four men throws three out of work. Of course, new industries are created and production increased to absorb part of the surplus labor, but sooner or later, we will reach the saturation point . . . and if we have reached it, there is only one solution, shorter working hours. Anything else will be suicidal."

And then, in October 1929, came the stock market crash. *Time* magazine said, "For so many months so many people had saved money and borrowed money and borrowed on their borrowings to possess themselves of the little pieces of paper by virtue of which they became partners in U.S. Industry [stocks certificates]. Now

The effect of the stock market crash was immediate. This Wall Street trader is selling his car for cash right after the October 1929 crash.

they were trying to get rid of them even more frantically than they had tried to get them."

The crash led to the worldwide Great Depression (1929–1942), the worst economic collapse in the history of the modern industrial world. Businesses failed, and over the next few years, more than 15 million Americans (one-quarter of the workforce) lost their jobs. Half of all African American workers were out of work. Without jobs, families could not afford to pay for their homes and for food. Many families became homeless and went hungry. To make matters worse, huge dust storms turned parts of Kansas, Colorado, Oklahoma, Texas, and New Mexico into a near desert. People from these states headed west hoping for jobs in California.

Dust storms throughout the south central and southwestern United States deepened the Great Depression. This dust cloud is engulfing a town in Colorado in 1934.

This California family ended up in a tent community outside of Los Angeles.

Many of them drove in cars piled high with chairs and beds and children. Others hitched rides in railroad boxcars. Jobs were scarce in California too, and many people ended up in makeshift tent communities.

## BROTHER, CAN YOU SPARE A DIME?

Charities or public welfare agencies provided only limited relief, so jobless men went "on the bum," drifting from state to state, riding the rails, seeking work or at least a handout. Homeless men would knock on back doors to ask for a meal or perhaps for old clothes and shoes. Most people were not afraid to answer the door to strangers, did not fear these men, and fed them if there was any food to spare. They believed, "What you give to the poor, you lend to the Lord."

Young American women had even fewer employment choices than men did. As one of them said sadly, "Today is my birthday, and I don't even have a nickel to buy an ice-cream cone." Ice cream cones really did cost a nickel then, a loaf of bread cost seven cents, milk was ten cents a quart, and ground beef sold for thirteen cents a pound. Yet people couldn't afford to buy these things, and they went hungry. They wore shoes till the soles had holes and then patched them with bits of leather or stuffed them with cardboard. Since most Americans had little money to spend, unsold goods piled up on store shelves. This forced hundreds of mills and factories to shut down.

## THE NEW DEAL

With the election of Franklin Delano Roosevelt (FDR) as president in 1932, the country began to see an end to the hard times. Roosevelt created a number of government programs—known as the New Deal—to get the nation back to work. One, the Civilian Conservation Corps (CCC),

President Franklin Roosevelt *(seated, fifth from left)* visits a camp for Civilian Conservation Corps (CCC) workers in 1933. Behind the president and his cabinet members are young men employed by the CCC program.

put young men to work building roads and clearing forest trails. In a radio address, Roosevelt said, "First, we are giving opportunity of employment to one-quarter of a million of the unemployed, especially the young men who have dependents, to go into the forestry and flood prevention work." In addition, Roosevelt created the Works Progress Administration (WPA). WPA workers built roads, bridges, and airport runways. Artists, musicians, actors, and writers participated in the Federal Theater Project and the Federal Writers' Project.

For the jobless, Franklin Roosevelt was a source of hope. Correspondent Martha Gellhorn wrote, "Every house I visited—mill worker or unemployed—had a picture of the President. These ranged from newspaper clippings to large colored prints. . . . He is at once God and their intimate friend; he knows them all by name, knows their little town and mill, their little lives and problems . . . and will not let them down."

## HOPE FOR UNIONS

FDR was also friendly to unions. He said, "If I went to work in a factory, the first thing I'd do would be to join a union. . . . It is one of the characteristics of a free and democratic nation that it have free and independent labor unions." Roosevelt's leadership brought the greatest gains the unions had won up to that time. The National Labor Relations Act (NLRA) of 1935 guaranteed workers, especially in mass-production industries such as steel and automaking, "the right to self-organization, to form, join, or assist labor organizations, to bargain collectively through representatives of their own choosing, and to engage in concerted activities for the purpose of collective bargaining or other mutual aid and protection." The act (also known as the Wagner Act for one of the senators who sponsored it) encouraged collective bargaining between workers and employers. Still strikes continued, more than at any time in U.S. history. Between May 1933 and July 1937, ten thousand strikes involved about 5.6 million workers. There were strikes by farmworkers, miners, textile workers, lumbermen, autoworkers, and others, usually because business owners had cut workers' hours and reduced their hourly pay rates.

## A NEW UNION

On November 9, 1935, United Mine Workers president John L. Lewis joined with the heads of seven other unions to form the Congress of Industrial Organization (CIO). Elected president of the CIO, Lewis reached out not just to the trade unionists traditionally represented by the AFL but to all workers in all the mass-production industries, including steel, electrical, automobile, maritime, transit, textile, and more. Industrial workers, who had no other union representation, joined this new union.

The AFL, the representative of trade unions, objected. The following August, American Federation of Labor officials told their union members to either withdraw from the CIO or get out of the AFL. The result was that, by 1937, the CIO had more members than the AFL.

At first the CIO had to beg for funding from its richest member, the United Mineworkers of America. And because it needed experienced organizers, the CIO recruited a number of long-term Communist Party activists. Putting forth a massive effort to reelect Franklin Roosevelt, the CIO helped FDR win a second term in 1936 by a landslide. Roosevelt had further earned the support of labor by spon-

United Mine Workers president John L. Lewis *(right)* talks with a member of the U.S. House of Representatives about labor issues in the 1920s.

soring historic, labor-friendly legislation such as Social Security (a government pension plan for retired workers), unemployment insurance for those out of work, and a federal minimum wage.

## BIG STEEL, LITTLE STEEL

Even with gains for labor, tensions with management led to conflict. For example, steel companies were openly hostile to the CIO, which was organizing steelworkers. United States Steel Corporation, in particular, wanted its employees to remain in the company unions. These separate craft unions operated inside the plants, where management could more easily control them. Craft union members were still mostly white male workers born in the United States—almost no women, foreign-born workers, or African Americans belonged. By contrast, the CIO industrial unionists wanted to unite all workers in each industry, skilled and unskilled, into a single organization.

The CIO welcomed men, women, blacks, non-English speakers, and even a few still-active Communists. They promised workers they'd have the power to negotiate as one big union within an industry instead of as a collection of smaller individual groups organized by a trade or skill. They could think of themselves as autoworkers, steelworkers, or miners, and not just as machinists or electricians or steamfitters. Setting out to organize the steel industry, the CIO formed the Steel Workers Organizing Committee (SWOC). Enough workers joined SWOC that U.S. Steel agreed to negotiate with the union. Union members won a pay raise to five dollars for an eight-hour day, with extra pay for overtime.

That ended Big Steel's nonunion policy, which had been in place since the Homestead Strike of 1892. But the smaller steel companies—referred to as Little Steel—refused to negotiate with SWOC. So in May 1937, eighty-five thousand workers struck at three separate Little Steel companies, including Republic Steel's South Chicago plant.

A paper in the Chicago History Museum describes the strike at Republic Steel: "May 30, Memorial Day, was a sunny, hot day with afternoon

Striking steelworkers wait in a CIO-sponsored breadline during the 1937 Little Steel Strike.

temperatures reaching 88 degrees. By 3:00 P.M., a crowd of around 1500 strikers and sympathizers had gathered. . . . About 15 percent of the crowd was made up of women and children." The crowd applauded loudly when a speaker mentioned President Roosevelt and John L. Lewis and urged workers to support the right to organize. Marching behind two American flags, about one thousand people moved toward the Republic Steel Plant, chanting, "CIO, CIO!" When they reached the gates of the plant, police attacked the marchers with billy clubs and gunfire. Ten marchers were shot to death, and thirty others suffered gunshot wounds. Sympathetic protesters clogged the business district in South Chicago. Angry strikers were almost ready to proclaim war against the police. Placing blame on the marchers, the *Chicago Tribune* said they "had attacked the police with clubs, bricks, and guns in a plan to get into the plant and throw out the non-union workers." But later, a U.S. government committee disagreed with the *Tribune*, saying "the marchers' provocation of the police did not go beyond the use of abusive language and the throwing of isolated missiles; and that the force used by the police to disperse the crowd was far in excess of that required." The CIO's strike failed. Republic Steel refused all of their demands.

## A COMMUNIST, A FASCIST, OR A SOCIALIST

That same spring, another union confrontation took place at a Ford plant in Dearborn, Michigan. Henry Ford wanted no unions in his automobile plants. He believed he treated his workers more than fairly, like a father protecting his sons. Certain workers, though, wanted to shake off Ford's paternalistic (fatherlike) control. On May 27, Walter Reuther, who headed a United Automobile Workers local union, approached the Ford plant gate with three other union organizers to ask for permission to hand out leaflets titled, "Unionism, not Fordism." An article in the Reuther Library at Wayne State University in Indiana reports, "Reuther and his companions were told to leave, [they were] allowed no time to respond or withdraw and [were] immediately attacked by the Ford thugs. They were punched, kicked, and picked up, slammed to the ground repeatedly, and after a severe beating, tossed down the stairs to the road below."

Reporters wrote about the attack, and photographers took pictures of the beatings and violence. Curtis Hanson writes in *The Battle of the Overpass*, "The testimony given by the outside observers, the medical people who treated the injured, and especially the widespread publication of the photographs swayed public opinion in favor of the UAW and left Ford facing new attitudes about his company. Also, as a result of this episode, his first appearance on the national stage, Walter Reuther emerged as an important leader within the UAW." Reuther went on to become president of the United Auto Workers Union.

## WORLD WAR II

In 1939 World War II (1939–1945) began in Europe. After the Japanese attacked Pearl Harbor, Hawaii, in December 1941, the United States joined the Allies (including Great Britain and France) and declared war on both Japan and Germany. U.S. factories quickly began to produce war materials for the U.S. military.

Millions of men and women joined the armed forces, and millions more went to work in industry, making good money for the first time since the start of the Great Depression. During World War II, 43 percent of all Americans worked in a factory, warehouse, mill, mine, or at some other blue-collar (manual labor) job. According to a recent government report, "World War Two was a metal-turning, engine-building, multiyear conflict that required an enormous amount of manual labor."

Those jobs included women, who went to work in the factories in greater numbers than ever before. Trade unions supported women's right to equal pay for equal work, to protect male members who might lose their jobs if women were willing to work for less. In 1944, at a United Auto Workers conference of women workers, members requested the union's support for maternity leave and child care. It didn't happen. Millie Jeffrey, the first head of the UAW's Women's Bureau, recalled, "The policies of the UAW were always very good. Getting them implemented [put into practice] was another story."

When employers began to fire women workers at the end of the war, unions, including the UAW, raised few objections. By 1947 the number of women in blue-collar jobs was back to the pre-war level.

Soon after Pearl Harbor, President Roosevelt brought together labor union leaders and business leaders to form the National War Labor Board to prevent labor disputes that might slow production.

These women went to work as welders during World War II. More women worked in factories during World War II than at any previous time.

Both sides were asked to pledge a no-strike no-lockout agreement. (In a lockout, management closes a business or factory to resist the demands of the unions.) Seizing the opportunity, union leaders used the wartime labor shortage (due to the draft and enlistments, which put many workers into the armed services to fight overseas) to force reluctant employers to recognize their unions. In return, the union leaders agreed not to strike during the war.

That pledge didn't keep workers from walking off the job in wild-cat strikes. In 1943 John L. Lewis's United Mine Workers closed down the nation's coal mines four times because their wages weren't keeping up with the increasing costs of living, in spite of many hours of over-time work. These wildcat strikes made Americans angry with the unions. Many people felt that strikes were unpatriotic in a time of war. Yet union membership grew by close to two-thirds from 1939 to 1945, from about 9 million to 15 million workers.

Conditions appeared to improve for workers after the war came to an end with an Allied victory. Wages rose as production of civilian goods increased. And as Ford knew, higher pay meant workers could buy more of what the factories produced. This made workers and owners so-called "partners in production." Strikes still took place, but labor and management made more attempts at arbitration and made more compromises to find solutions and keep down violence.

## THE COLD WAR

In the postwar years, political tension between the United States and its former ally, the Soviet Union, intensified into a nonmilitary conflict known as the Cold War (1945–1991). Americans feared and distrusted Soviet Communism, and labor leaders such as UAW's Walter Reuther worked to purge Communists from the unions. Because of this anti-Communist crusade and because of his efforts to rid unions of corruption, Reuther was often a target of violence. In April 1948, he was shot at in his own kitchen. "It could have been [by] management, a Communist, a Fascist or a screwball. I can't put them in any order," he said. Though his right arm was severely injured, Reuther declared, "The momentum and power of our new kind of labor movement cannot be stopped and thrown back by slugs from a shotgun."

A failed bomb attempt at UAW headquarters in 1950 might have been because of Reuther's anti-Communist crusade. Or it might have been because of his attempt to stamp out illegal gambling operations in one of the auto plants. Theories abound about the bombing and about the airplane crash that killed Walter Reuther in 1970. The FBI still refuses to make public nearly two hundred pages of documents about Reuther's death.

## UNIONS AND ORGANIZED CRIME

As the economy boomed in the 1950s, organized labor also gained ground. In 1955 two of the largest U.S. labor organizations, the AFL and the CIO merged to form the AFL-CIO. Former AFL chief George Meany became head of the AFL-CIO, with 15 million members.

In 1957 the organization expelled its largest member union, the Teamsters, because of corruption. The 1.5 million-member Teamsters Union was made up mostly of highway truck drivers. It was led by James R. (Jimmy) Hoffa and other officials who had connections to organized crime. A congressional committee reported that the union

George Meany *(standing left)* and Walter Reuther *(standing right)* strike the gavel as they announce the merger of the AFL and CIO to create the AFL-CIO in 1955.

and Hoffa were guilty of "squandered and stolen union funds, sweetheart contracts, conflicts of interest among employers and labor leaders, phony paper locals and denial of democratic process to members, collusions and coercions and violence always about to break out" in cities across the country, including New York, Chicago, Detroit, Cleveland, Saint Louis, Pittsburgh, and Minneapolis. (A sweetheart contract is an agreement that benefits an employer and union officials but doesn't help workers. Paper locals are local unions started by union officials that have no actual members.)

A decade later, Hoffa went to prison for attempting to bribe a federal jury. His sentence was commuted (exchanged for a less severe penalty) by President Richard Nixon with the condition that Hoffa leave the Teamsters. Hoffa not only resigned, he disappeared. His body has never been found.

Jimmy Hoffa *(left)* replaced Dave Beck *(right)* as president of the Teamsters Union in 1957. Here the two talk at a Teamsters meeting. Both men were convicted of participating in illegal activities during their time as president of the Teamsters Union.

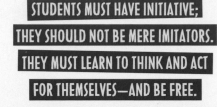

# CHAPTER EIGHT

# THE FACES OF AMERICAN WORKERS

The family of Cesar Chavez (1927–1993) lost its farm in Arizona during the Depression. To survive, they moved to California and traveled through the state picking crops in the fields, earning very little. As Cesar grew up, he saw that fruit growers, to keep wages low, illegally bused Mexican workers across the U.S. border to work in the fields. Housing was shabby and overcrowded, often with no running water, heat, or electricity. Workers often had to buy supplies in stores owned by the growers, falling into debt to them—as earlier, coal miners had fallen into debt in the coal company stores. The farmworkers had no right to form labor unions. They had no Social Security, unemployment insurance, or guaranteed minimum wage. Instead of going to school, children of migrant workers often worked beside their parents in the fields.

In the 1960s, Cesar Chavez and Dolores Huerta organized the United Farm Workers Association to help all migrant workers gain higher wages and better living conditions. But their strikes often failed, because as Chavez explained, "The employers go to Mexico and have unlimited, unrestricted use of illegal alien strikebreakers to break the strike. And for over 30 years, the Immigration and Naturalization Service [a U.S. agency dealing with immigration issues] has looked the other way and assisted in the strikebreaking. I do not remember one single instance in 30 years where the Immigration Service has removed strikebreakers. . . . The employers use professional smugglers to recruit and transport human contraband [illegal goods] across the Mexican border for the specific act of strikebreaking."

Cesar Chavez *(center, with sign)* pickets with other members of the United Farm Workers Association in Califonia during the 1960s.

In a brilliant move, Chavez called for a nationwide boycott of grapes until the grape pickers were given decent wages. Dolores Huerta worked as East Coast coordinator. The AFL-CIO and the United Auto Workers supported the farmworkers and the boycott spread. Millions of Americans stopped buying grapes. Finally, the vineyard owners agreed to offer the workers health insurance and a raise in pay. A few years later, the United Farm Workers Association joined the AFL-CIO. Huerta then headed the political arm of the farmworkers' union, lobbying Congress for workers' protections.

Martin Luther King Jr. speaks to the press in New York, New York, shortly before leaving for Memphis, Tennessee, in 1968. There he supported striking sanitation workers.

In 1968 thirteen hundred sanitation workers, most of them African Americans, went on strike in Memphis, Tennessee, to protest low wages and poor working conditions. Civil rights leader Martin Luther King Jr. traveled to Memphis to support these workers. There, on April 3, he gave his last civil rights speech, urging his listeners to march with the strikers and to support them in their battle for fair treatment. He warned that unless they all stood together, all of them would face defeat. The next evening, April 4, King was standing on the balcony of his motel room when a shot rang out. King, who preached nonviolence, became the victim of a sniper's bullet. Only days after his death, King's bereaved widow, Coretta Scott King, returned to Memphis to march with the sanitation workers, who soon won recognition for their union, the American Federation of State, County and Municipal Employees (AFSCME). They also demanded and won wage increases and an end to racial discrimination in promotions and job assignments.

## GOING GLOBAL

By the late 1970s, foreign competition led U.S. businesses to demand concessions from unions. In the steel industry, for example, imports of cheaper foreign steel made the industry less profitable. By the early 1980s, U.S. Steel had laid off one hundred thousand workers and had shut down 150 steel mills across the country. One was the Duquesne Works in Pennsylvania. This was the mill Andrew Carnegie had bought in 1890 after spreading rumors that its products were inferior. On the day the mill closed, a bugler played taps over the mill's public address system. One steelworker lamented, "Duquesne without the steel mill is like a man without a soul."

In 1981 U.S. unions were dealt a blow that was felt for the next decades. The Professional Air Traffic Controllers Organization (PATCO) went on strike for higher pay. But as *Newsweek* magazine noted, "controllers concede [admit that] their chief complaint was not money, but hours, working conditions, and a lack of recognition for the pressures they face" directing airplanes through takeoffs and landings and protecting safety in the skies. President Ronald Reagan noted that PATCO was a government union and that government unions had a no-strike clause in their contracts. When the air traffic controllers stayed off the job, Reagan told the Federal Aviation Administration to fire 11,345 of the strikers and to hire replacements. Only about 500 PATCO members were ever rehired. The rest were permanently blackballed from the industry.

Some scholars believe that the PATCO firings helped mark the beginning of the decline of labor unions in the United States. And indeed, the 1980s continued with harder times for organized labor. Membership dropped from 20 percent to 12 percent of the work force. And to further reduce costs to compete with overseas manufacturers, U.S. employers began to use temporary and part-time workers, who did not belong to unions. As more union members lost jobs and benefits, their leaders searched for ways to deal with these economic changes.

## PUBLIC SECTOR UNIONS

In the early history of labor, unions included workers in goods-producing jobs. Unions eventually saw the need to also represent workers in the service industries, which include banking, transportation, health care, hotels, restaurants, and computer repair. In modern times, the Service Employees International Union (SEIU) represents employees in health care (nurses and nursing home employees), public services (schoolteachers and other government employees), building services (janitors and security guards),

State employees and their families gather in Madison, Wisconsin, to protest planned layoffs in the early 2000s. The president of the American Federation of State, County and Municipal Employees (AFSCME) union is speaking from the podium.

and others. The SEIU has grown in membership over the years, from 625,000 members in 1980 to nearly 2 million members at the end of 2007. The American Federation of State, County and Municipal Employees union is another major public sector union that includes workers in various government jobs and has a membership of about 1.4 million.

## NAFTA

The North American Free Trade Agreement (NAFTA) went into effect on the first of January 1994. This treaty was meant to increase trade among the United States, Mexico, and Canada by reducing the tariffs (taxes) added to goods shipped and sold across international borders.

Many people disagree about the impact of free-trade agreements such as NAFTA. For example, John Edwards, a Democratic senator from the manufacturing state of North Carolina, commented, "Since these agreements were put into place we have lost millions of manufacturing jobs, seen wages decline, and storied U.S. firms close—and towns all over this country have been devastated. And we have run up larger and larger trade deficits. . . . NAFTA, which was one of our worst trade agreements ever, was written by corporate interests and insiders in all three countries, and it has served them well. But it absolutely hasn't served the interests of regular workers in any of the three countries. . . ." Other people have pointed out, however, that many of the problems in manufacturing have little to do with NAFTA and more to do with an increasingly competitive global marketplace and with internal problems in some of the hardest-hit companies, such as auto manufacturing.

In recent years, many thousands of U.S. jobs have been lost to outsourcing—sending jobs overseas to be done more cheaply by workers in India, China, the Philippines, and other countries. Yet even as U.S. jobs moved across oceans, immigrants—many of them undocumented—have come in large numbers over the Mexican-U.S. border to take low-paying agricultural, manufacturing, and hospitality jobs that companies have trouble filling with domestic labor. One idea

Outsourcing labor for U.S. companies has become increasingly common in the 2000s. The workers above are based in Mumbai, India.

proposed to deal with the situation is to expand a guest worker program for Mexicans and other undocumented workers in the United States. *Time* magazine predicted, "For many factories, guest workers can do little more than delay the inevitable shutdown that comes from dying demand or global competition." The issue of immigrant labor remains highly controversial in the United States, and solutions remain difficult to achieve.

Facing increasingly emotional debate about immigration, both documented and undocumented immigrants demonstrate in Los Angeles, California, to raise awareness about immigrant labor in the United States.

## THE CHANGING FACE OF UNIONS

In 2005 two of the nation's largest and most powerful unions resigned from the AFL-CIO. One was the 1.3 million-member Teamsters Union. The other was the 1.9 million-member SEIU. These two unions split from the AFL-CIO because, said SEIU president Andrew L. Stern, "Our world has changed, our economy has changed, employers have changed. But the AFL-CIO is not willing to make fundamental changes." The SEIU's goals are for "each worker to gain a paycheck that supports a family, to give workers a voice on the job, to obtain universal health care and a secure retirement, and to truly reflect the diversity of today's workforce." To work toward these goals, SEIU has joined with six other unions that are not part of the AFL-CIO.

On the other hand, the National Education Association (NEA)—a teachers' union—became partners with the AFL-CIO the next year. This agreement allows the teachers' state and local unions to join the AFL-CIO's state and local labor councils. The NEA is the nation's largest professional employee organization, representing 3.2 million elementary and secondary teachers, higher education faculty, education support professionals, school administrators, retired educators, and students preparing to become teachers. "By giving NEA local members the opportunity to unite with our members," said AFL-CIO president John Sweeney, "we'll be able to wage stronger campaigns to help working families fend off escalating assaults on family incomes, education, health care, pensions, and public services. And we'll be stronger in the fight for quality, affordable health care for all, retirement security, and a great education for our children." Another teachers' union, the American Federation of Teachers (AFT), is also affiliated with the AFL-CIO. The AFT has 1.4 million members.

In an effort to remain vital and to attract new members, some unions have begun to reach out to immigrant workers. The number of immigrants, documented and undocumented, represented by unions surged to 2 million in 2006, up from 1.6 million ten years earlier. In 2007 in New

York City, a number of Chinese workers, some without legal immigration papers, had jobs riding bicycles through the city's traffic to deliver restaurant food. They had been earning less than half the minimum wage of $5.85 an hour, and some earned as little as $1.60 an hour. With the support of the Restaurant Workers Union, thirty of these delivery workers banded together to unionize and to wage a strike. Hundreds of delivery workers, waiters, cooks, and bus staff from across New York joined their picket lines in a show of solidarity. "We began to sense that maybe we were not helpless, that maybe even people like us could fight for our rights," said one of the delivery workers, an immigrant from China who had arrived illegally in the United States twelve years earlier. "We feel strong now," he said. "And that feels good."

## THE FUTURE

By the end of 2006, the percentage of the U.S. workforce represented by unions had fallen from 16.5 million to 14.8 million over the previous ten years. Labor unions are facing new challenges, such as the rising cost of health benefits for retired workers and higher pay for service workers in low-paying jobs. These service workers are being urged to join unions to gain a decent wage. In 2007 the number of American workers belonging to labor unions rose for the first time in a quarter century. Union membership increased that year by 311,000, to 15.7 million members, and growth was especially high in construction and health care. In addition, more than 201,000 women joined unions in 2007, nearly twice the number of men who joined. Women account for 44 percent of all union members, a new high. This upward trend in union membership is good news for union leaders who had been expecting a drop in membership because of a loss of jobs in manufacturing, especially in the auto industry. "I don't think the number means we've turned the corner," said Tom Woodruff, executive vice president in charge of organizing at the SEIU. "I think it's significant the labor movement is growing. But it's not nearly enough."

Overall, the biggest recent gains in union membership are in government, where 37 percent of federal, state, and local government employees belong to unions. Local governments, with 42 percent union participation, have the highest union membership in public service jobs.

AFL-CIO president Sweeney comments on the overall trend by noting that "today's numbers show working people are pushing to form and join unions in order to improve their lives, despite record levels of resistance from employers. They know that a union card is the single best ticket into the middle class, especially in today's economy." The advantages of having a union on the job could be seen in 2007 when the average weekly pay for union members was $863, while nonunion workers earned an average of $663 per week.

Mark H. Ayers, president of the Building and Construction Trades Department, AFL-CIO, believes, "This increase in membership and union market share is a direct result of the aggressive marketing, organizing and recruitment efforts undertaken by our affiliated unions. And this is just the beginning."

In 2008 Andy Stern, the president of SEIU, said, "America still needs strong unions—as well as a government on the side of working people—as part of the solution to rebalance power, provide greater fairness, make work pay and ensure that the dreams of all American children can still come true."

The coming years will prove if he's right.

In the 2000s, the concerns of labor organizations are changing along with changes in technology. For example, in late 2007, the Writers Guild of America went on strike (*above*) to secure compensation for screenwriters' work offered on the Internet.

They called it the "trial of the century." The defendant was William Haywood of the Western Federation of Miners, a union with a reputation for violence. Haywood had been accused of masterminding the murder of former Idaho governor Frank Steunenburg, who'd called out federal troops against striking silver miners in the northern part of the state. (In 2007 the Haywood trial was reenacted for a public television special.)

The jury consisted of twelve bewhiskered Idaho farmers, all of them expected to be hostile to labor unions. But as defense counsel Clarence Darrow made his plea, the jurors listened closely. Darrow said:

> Let me tell you, gentlemen, if you destroy the labor unions in this country, you destroy liberty when you strike the blow, and you would leave the poor bound and shackled and helpless to do the bidding of the rich . . . . It would take this country back . . . to the time when there were masters and slaves.

> I don't mean to tell this jury that labor organizations do no wrong. I know them too well for that. They do wrong often, and sometimes brutally; they are sometimes cruel; they are often unjust; they are frequently corrupt. . . . But I am here to say that in a great cause these labor organizations, despised and weak and outlawed as they generally are, have stood for the poor, they have stood for the weak, they have stood for every human law that was ever placed upon the statute books. They stood for human life, they stood for the father who was bound down by his task, they stood for the wife, threatened to be taken from the home to work by his side, and they have stood for the little child who was also taken to work in their places—that the rich could grow richer still, and they have fought for

Clarence Darrow *(standing)* addresses the court during the trial of Bill Haywood *(third from right)* in 1907.

the right of the little one, to give him a little of life, a little comfort while he is young. I don't care how many wrongs they committed, I don't care how many crimes these weak, rough, rugged, unlettered men who often know no other power but the brute force of their strong right arm, who find themselves bound and confined and impaired whichever way they turn, who look up and worship the god of might as the only god that they know—I don't care how often they fail, how many brutalities they are guilty of. I know their cause is just.

Perhaps the biggest impact on the jury came from this one sentence Clarence Darrow then said: "Had it not been for the trade unions of the world, you today would be serfs instead of free men."

The foreman of the jury handed the judge the envelope. He opened it and passed the paper inside to the court clerk to read aloud. William Haywood was declared not guilty.

6   Julian P. Boyd, ed. *Papers of Thomas Jefferson*, vol. 11 (Princeton, NJ: Princeton University Press, 1955), 93, also available online at http://www.monticello.org/library/reference/famquote.html (April 16, 2008).

8   American Council for Polish Culture, "Poles at Jamestown," *Polish News*, n.d., http://old.polishnews.com/system/main.php?a=text/news_and_correspondence/poles_at_jamestown (April 10, 2008).

9   Ibid.

10   Frank E. Smitha, "The French Revolution," *Macrohistory and World Report*, 2002, http://www.fsmitha.com/h3/h33-fr.html (April 12, 2008).

11   Marcus Rediker, *Between the Devil and the Deep Blue Sea* (Cambridge: Cambridge University Press, 1987), 110.

11   U.S. History Encyclopedia, "Strikes," *Answers.com,* n.d., http://www.answers.com/topic/strike?cat=bizfin&nr=1 (April 11, 2008).

12   Wythe Holt, *Labor Conspiracy Cases in the United States, 1805–1842,* in Omar Swarts, "Defending Labor in Commonwealth v. Pullis: Contemporary Implications for Rethinking Community," *eLaw Journal* 14, no. 2 (March 2004): 613-615, available online at *Murdoch University Electronic Journal of Law* vol. 11, no. 1 (March 2004), http://www.murdoch.edu.au/elaw/issues/v11n1/swartz111.html (April 11, 2008).

13   "Recollections of Slavery by a Runaway Slave" in *Emancipator,* 1838, available online at *Documenting the American South*, March 12, 2008, http://docsouth.unc.edu/neh/runaway/runaway.html (April 11, 2008).

16   Harriet Hanson Robinson, *Loom and Spindle; or, Life among the Early Mill Girls* (1898, reprt., Kailua, HI: Press Pacifica, 1976), available online at http://courses.wcupa.edu/johnson/robinson.html (April 11, 2008).

19   John Babsone Lane Soule, *Terre Haute (IN) Express*, 1851.

20–21   Abraham Lincoln, *The Writings of Abraham Lincoln*, available online at *Classic Literature Library*, n.d., http://www.classic-literature.co.uk/american-authors/19th-century/abraham-lincoln/the-writings-of-abraham-lincoln-05/ebook-page-64.asp (April 11, 2008).

23    James B. Fry, "Report of Col. James B. Fry. Provost-Marshall-General, U.S. Army, with Orders, gc," *Civilwarhome.com*, October 6, 2001, http://www.civilwarhome.com/fryor.htm (April 11, 2008).

24    Philip S. Foner, ed., *History of the Labor Movement in the United States: From the Founding of the American Federation of Labor to the Emergence of American Imperialism*, vol. 2 (New York: International Publisher, 1955), 110.

25    Beth Gibson, "The First Transcontinental Railroad," *AOL Hometown*, December 13, 2006, http://members.aol.com/Gibson0817/cp-up.htm (April 11, 2008).

25    Sierra College, "Central Pacific Railroad Timeline," *Sierra Nevada Virtual Museum*, n.d., http://www.sierranevadavirtualmuseum.com/docs/galleries/history/transportation/centralpacific.htm (April 11, 2008).

27    Michael Woodiwiss, *Organized Crime and American Power: A History* (Toronto: University of Toronto Press, 2001), 122.

28    Ted Nace, *Gangs of America: The Rise of Corporate Power and the Disabling of Democracy* (San Francisco: Berrett-Koehler Publishers, 2003), 65.

28    *Harper's Weekly*, "The Great Strike," August 11, 1877, available online at *Catskill Archive*, 2000–2005, http://catskillarchive.com/rrextra/sk7711.Html (April 11, 2008).

28    *Chicago Times*, July 26, 1877.

29    Karl Marx, quoted in "Free Trade and Protectionism," *Marxists.org*, n.d., http://www.marxists.org/glossary/terms/f/r.htm (April 12, 2008).

30    George Woodcock, *Anarchism: A History of Libertarian Ideas and Movements* (Calgary: Broadview Press, 2004), 396.

30–31  Philip S. Foner, *The Autobiographies of the Haymarket Martyrs* (New York: Pathfinder Press, 1977), 6.

31    Ibid., 11.

32    WITF, "Making Steel," *ExplorePAhistory.com*, 2003, http://www.explorepahistory.com/story.php?storyId=27&chapter=4 (April 11, 2008).

32    Andrew Carnegie, quoted in "Andrew Carnegie," *Quoteworld.org*, 2008, http://www.quoteworld.org/quotes/9944 (April 11, 2008).

32 Andrew Carnegie, quoted in "Andrew Carnegie," *Quoteworld.org*, 2008, http://www.quoteworld.org/authors/andrew-carnegie (April 11, 2008).

32 Andrew Carnegie, quoted in "Andrew Carnegie Quotes," *BrainyQuote.com*, 2008, http://www.brainyquote.com/quotes/authors/a/andrew_carnegie.html (April 11, 2008).

34 William Serrin, *Homestead: The Glory and Tragedy of an American Steel Town* (New York: Times Books, 1992), 50.

35 Ibid., 71.

35 Ibid., 73.

36 *Illustrated American*, "The Incident of the 6th of July," July 16, 1892, *ehistory*, 2008, http://ehistory.osu.edu/osu/mmh/HomesteadStrike1892/HistoryofSevenDays/incident.cfm (April 11, 2008).

36 PBS, "Strike at Homestead Mill," *PBS Online*, 1999, http://www.pbs.org/wgbh/amex/carnegie/sfeature/mh_horror.html (April 11, 2008).

38 Henry Clay Frick, quoted in "Emma Goldman," *PBS Online*, 2004, http://www.pbs.org/wgbh/amex/goldman/peopleevents/p_frick.html (April 11, 2008).

38 Emma Goldman, quoted in "Emma Goldman," *PBS Online*, 2004, http://www.pbs.org/wgbh/amex/goldman/peopleevents/p_goldman.html (April 11, 2008).

39–40 Dick Meister, "Labor—and a Whole Lot More, the Great Pullman Strike," *DickMeister.com*, n.d., http://dickmeister.com/id71.html (April 11, 2008).

40 Albert Fried, ed., *Socialism in America: From the Shakers to the Third International* (New York: Columbia University Press, 1992), 466.

43 "Wire from Emma Goldman," *New York Times*, July 30, 1907.

44 Henry Ford, quoted in "Henry Ford quotes," *ThinkExist.com*, 2006, http://thinkexist.com/quotes/henry_ford/4.html (April 11, 2008).

44 George Gorham Groat, *An Introduction to the Study of Organized Labor* (New York: Macmillan Company, 1916), 450.

45 Samuel Gompers, quoted in "Samuel Gompers," *Illinois Labor History Society*, n.d., http://www.kentlaw.edu/ilhs/gompers.htm (April 14, 2008).

45 Samuel Gompers, quoted in "Samuel Gompers Quotes," *BrainyQuote.com*, 2008, http://www.brainyquote.com/quotes/quotes/s/ samuelgomp205268.html (April 11, 2008).

47 Anonymous, quoted in *Outlook Magazine*, available online in Joyce Korn- bluh, "Bread and Roses: The 1912 Lawrence Textile Strike," *The Lucy Parsons Project*, September 17, 2005, http://www.lucyparsonsproject.org/iww/korn- bluh_bread_roses.html (April 11, 2008).

48 Arnold Dosch, "What the I.W.W. Is," *World's Work* 26, no. 4 (August 1913): 406–420, available online at *Jim Crutchfield's I.W.W. Page*, January 7, 2005, http:// www.workerseducation.org/crutch/others/dosch.html (April 11, 2008).

51 Joyce Kornbluh, *Rebel Voices: An IWW Anthology* (Chicago: Charles H. Kerr Publishing, 1988), 162.

51 Elizabeth Gurley Flynn, *The Rebel Girl: An Autobiography, My First Life (1906–1926)* (New York: International Publishers Co., 1973), 132.

52 James Oppenheim, "Bread and Roses," *American Magazine*, December 1911, 214.

52 William D. Haywood, as quoted in William Moran, *The Belles of New Eng- land* (New York: St. Martin's Press, 2002) 216.

53 *New York Times*, March 26, 1911, 1, 4.

53 Ibid.

56 Mary Harris Jones, *The Autobiography of Mother Jones*, ed. Mary Field Parton (Mineola, NY: Courier Dover Publications, 2004), 120.

56 Clayton Sinyai, *Schools of Democracy, a Political History of the American Labor Movement* (Ithaca, NY: Cornell University Press, 2006), 36.

57 Ace Collins, *The Stories behind Country Music's All-Time Greatest: 100 Song* (New York: Boulevard Books, 1996), 91–93.

58 Jones, *The Autobiography*, 113.

58 Jack London, *Jack London: American Rebel* (New York: Citadel, 1947), 57.

61 Colorado Bar Association, "Historical Foreward and Bibliography," *CBA*, n.d., http://www.cobar.org/index.cfm/ID/581/dpwfp/ Historical-Foreward-and-Bibliography (April 11, 2008).

62–63   John D. Rockefeller Jr., quoted in "The Ludlow Massacre," *PBS Online*, 2000, http://www.pbs.org/wgbh/amex/rockefellers/sfeature/ sf_8.html (April 11, 2008).

63   John Pettigrew and Dawn Keeley, *Public Women, Public Words: A Documentary History of American Feminism* (Lanham, MD: Rowman & Littlefield, 2002), 401–402.

64   PBS, "Teaching Guide," *Freedom: A History of Us,* n.d., http://www-tc.pbs .org/wnet/historyofus/teachers/pdfs/segment11-6.pdf (April 11, 2008).

65   George Burson, "US History Curriculum: Chapter X," *The James Madison History Center,* May 17, 2004, http://www.jmu.edu/madison/ center/main_pages/teacher/curriculum/chap10.htm (April 11, 2008).

65–66   "The U.S. Sedition Act," *World War I Document Archive,* August 4, 2007, http://wwi.lib.byu.edu/index.php/The_U.S._Sedition_Act (April 14, 2008).

66   *Milwaukee Leader,* April 23, 1921, 1.

66   Alix Holt and Barbara Holland, trans. *Theses Resolutions and Manifestos of the First Four Congresses of the Third International* (London: Ink Links, 1980), available online at *Marxists.org,* n.d., http://www.marxists.org/ history/international/comintern/3rd-congress/trade-unions.htm (April 11, 2008).

66   Vladimir Lenin, *Collected Works*, 1st English ed., vol. 32 (Moscow: Progress Publishers, 1965), 501.

67   Samuel Gompers, letter to J. H. Reiter, Archives of H. Keith Thompson, Hoover Institution, Stanford University.

68   Ella Mae Wiggins, "Mill Mother's Lament," *Marxist-Leninist Translations and Reprints,* n.d., http://www.mltranslations.org/US/Rpo/women/ iwwd1.htm (April 11, 2008).

68   Samuel Gompers, letter to J. H. Reiter, archives of H. Keith Thompson for the Thompson Collection in the Hoover Institution, available online at http://www.cwalocal4250.org/politicalaction/binarydata/ The%20Voice%20of%20Labor.pdf (April 14, 2008).

69 *Time,* "In New Orleans" December 3, 1928, available online at http://www.time.com/time/magazine/article/0,9171,928264,00.html?promoid=google (April 14, 2008).

69 Calvin Coolidge, *Have Faith in Massachusetts: A Collection of Speeches and Messages* (Boston: Houghton Mifflin Company, 1919), 198.

69 Ella Mae Wiggins, quoted in Roxanne Newton, "Blood on the Cloth: Ella May Wiggins and the 1929 Gastonia Strike," *North Carolina Humanities Council,* n.d., http://www.nchumanities.org/speaker/catalog25c.html (April 11, 2008).

70 Sinyai, *Schools of Democracy,* 70.

70 *Time,* "Deals, Financing," July 29, 1929, available online at http://www.time.com/time/magazine/article/0,9171,786083,00.html?iid=chix-sphere (April 11, 2008).

70–71 *Time,* "5,000,000 Jobless?" March 12, 1928, available online at http://www.time.com/time/magazine/article/0,9171,786310,00.html (April 11, 2008).

71 Ibid.

71 *Time,* "Bankers v. Panic," November 4, 1929, available online at http://www.time.com/time/magazine/article/0,9171,787517,00.html (April 11, 2008).

73 Serena Decker Flister, to the author, repeated often during the Great Depression.

73–74 Mae Decker Regensburger, to Serena Decker Flister, September 23, 1934.

75 Franklin Delano Roosevelt, "Second Fireside Chat," May 7, 1933, *The American Presidency Project,* 2008, http://www.presidency.ucsb.edu/ws/index.php?pid=14636 (April 11, 2008).

75 Martha Gelhorn, report, Gaston County, North Carolina, November 11, 1934, Franklin D. Roosevelt Library, Hopkins Papers, Box 66.

75 Franklin Delano Roosevelt, quoted on a CIO recruiting poster, 1936, available online at *e-workers,* n.d., http://www.ibew.org/eworkers/

organize/leaders.htm (April 11, 2008).

75    Franklin Delano Roosevelt, in a speech before the Teamsters Union, Washington, DC, September 11, 1940.

75    "National Labor Relations Act (1935)," *ourdocuments.gov*, n.d., http://www.ourdocuments.gov/doc.php?flash=true&doc=67 (April 11, 2008).

78    William Bork, "Massacre at Republic Steel" *Chicago Labor & Arts Festival Blog*, May 18, 2007, http://chilaborarts.wordpress.com/category/labor-history/ (April 11, 2008).

79    Ibid.

79    Curtis Hansen, "The Battle of the Overpass," *Walter P. Reuther Library, Wayne State University,* October 2005, http://www.reuther.wayne.edu/exhibits/battle.html (April 11, 2008).

79    Ibid.

80    Nelson Lichtenstein, "Labor and the Working Class in World War II," *National Historic Landmarks Program*, 2007, 88, available online at http://www.nps.gov/nhl/themes/Homefront/Part3.pdf (April 14, 2008).

80    Millie Jeffrey, as quoted in Nelson Lichtenstein, "Labor," 95.

81–82    *Time*, "Who Shot Walter?" May 3, 1948, available online at http://www.time.com/time/magazine/article/0,9171,798514,00.html (April 11, 2008).

82    Nelson Lichtenstein, *Walter Reuther, the Most Dangerous Man in Detroit* (Urbana: University of Illinois Press, 1997), 273.

83    CrimeLibrary, "Hoffa and the Mob," *Crimelibrary.com*, 2007, http://www.crimelibrary.com/notorious_murders/ famous/jimmy_hoffa/2.html (April 11, 2008).

84    Cesar Chavez, quoted in "Cesar Chavez Quotes," *Thinkexist.com,* 2006, http://thinkexist.com/quotes/cesar_chavez/2.html (April 11, 2008).

85    Cesar Chavez, quoted in Steve Sailer, "Cesar Chavez, Minuteman," *American Conservative*, February 27, 2006, http://www.amconmag.com/2006/2006_02_27/article.html (April 11, 2008).

87    *McKeesport (PA) Daily News*, May 1984

87  Rebecca Pels, "The Pressures of PATCO: Strikes and Stress in the 1980s," *Corcoran Department of History at the University of Virginia*, 1995, http://etext. virginia.edu/journals/EH/EH37/Pels.html (April 14, 2008).

89  John Edwards, "John Edwards's Statement on Peru Trade Agreement, October, 27, 2007," *Alliance for Responsible Trade*, 2007, http://www .art-us.org/node/282 (April 11, 2008).

90  *Time*, "Can a Guest Worker Program Work?" May 24, 2007, available online at http://www.time.com/time/magazine/article/0,9171,1625191-2,00. html (April 12, 2008).

91  Andrew L. Stern, "Statement by SEIU President," *SEIU*, July 25, 2005, http://www.seiu.net/media/pressreleases.cfm?pr_id=1238 (April 11, 2008).

91  James Parks, "N.Y. Teachers' Union Set to Merge," *AFL-CIO Now Blog*, May 18, 2006, http://blog.aflcio.org/2006/05/18/ ny-teachers%E2%80%99-unions-set-to-merge/ (April 11, 2008).

92  Anthony Faiola, "30 Immigrants on Bikes Deliver a Labor Revolt," *Washington Post*, August 25, 2007, A01.

92  Sholnn Freeman, "Union Membership Up Slightly in 2007," *Washington Post*, January 26, 2008, D02.

93  Steve Smith, "Union Membership Increased in 2007, According to Government Stats," *AFL-CIO*, January 25, 2008, http://www.aflcio .org/mediacenter/prsptm/pr01252008.cfm (April 12, 2008).

93  Mark H. Ayers, quoted in "Construction Union Membership Increases Dramatically in 2007," *Building and Construction Trades Department, AFL-CIO*, January 28, 2008, http://www.bctd.org/ newsroom/?subSec=13&id=111 (April 12, 2008).

93  Andy Stern, "Labor's New New Deal," *AlterNet*, March 24, 2008, http:// www.alternet.org/workplace/80472 (April 11, 2008).

AFL-CIO. "Unions of the AFL-CIO." *AFL-CIO.* 2008. http://www.aflcio.org/aboutus/unions/ (April 8, 2008).

American Labor Studies Center. "Welcome." *ALSC.* 2007. http://www.labor-studies.org/ (April 10, 2008).

Byington, Margaret F., *Homestead. The Households of a Mill Town.* Pittsburgh: University of Pittsburgh Press, 1974.

Foner, Philip S., ed. *The Autobiographies of the Haymarket Martyrs.* New York: Pathfinder Press, 1977.

Goldman, Emma. *Living My Life In Two Volumes, Volume One and Volume Two.* New York: Dover Publications, 1970.

Hakim, Joy. *A History of Us, Book Eight, an Age of Extremes, 1870–1917.* New York: Oxford University Press, 1999.

Jones, Mary Harris. *The Autobiography of Mother Jones.* Edited by Mary Field Parton. Mineola, NY: Courier Dover Publications, 2004.

LeBlanc, Paul. *A Short History of the U.S. Working Class.* New York: Humanity Books, 1999.

Leuchtenburg, William E. *The Perils of Prosperity 1914–32.* Chicago and London: University of Chicago Press, 1958.

Maine AFL-CIO. "Between a Rock and a Hard Place." *Labor Union History.* N.d. http://www.maineaflcio.org/labor_union_history.htm (April 8, 2008).

Miner, Curtis, *Homestead, The Story of a Steel Town.* Pittsburgh: Historical Society of Western Pennsylvania, 1989.

Rayback, Joseph G. *A History of American Labor.* New York: The Free Press, 1966.

Rose, James D. *Duquesne and the Rise of Steel Unionism.* Urbana and Chicago: University of Illinois Press, 2001.

Serrin, William. *Homestead, The Glory and Tragedy of an American Steel Town*. New York: Times Books, Random House, 1992.

Service Employees International Union. "About SEIU." *SEIU*. 2008. http://www.seiu.net/about/index.cfm (April 8, 2008).

Silverman, Jacob. "Labor Unions." *How Stuff Works*. N.d. http://money.howstuffworks.com/labor-union4.htm (April 8, 2008).

Sinyai, Clayton. *Schools of Democracy, a Political History of the American Labor Movement*. Ithaca, NY: Cornell University Press, 2006.

Union Web Services. "National Labor Unions." *Union Web Services*. 2005. http://www.unionwebservices.com/weblinks/labor_unions_in_the_us (April 10, 2008).

U.S. Department of Labor. "The History of Labor Day." *U.S. Department of Labor in the 21st Century*. March 19, 2008. http://www.dol.gov/opa/aboutdol/laborday.htm (April 8, 2008).

Watson, Bruce. *Bread and Roses: Mills, Migrants, and the Struggle for the American Dream*. New York: Viking, 2005.

Weisberger, Bernard A., ed. *The WPA Guide to America: The Best of 1930s American as Seen by the Federal Writers' Project*. New York: Pantheon Books, 1985.

# FURTHER READING AND WEBSITES

## BOOKS

Behnke, Alison. *Chinese in America*. Minneapolis: Twenty-First Century Books, 2005.

Brexel, Bernadette. *The Knights of Labor and the Haymarket Riot*. New York: Rosen, 2003.

Collins, David R. *Farmerworker's Friend: The Story of Cesar Chavez*. Minneapolis: Twenty-First Century Books, 1996.

Goldstein, Margaret J. *Irish in America*. Minneapolis: Twenty-First Century Books, 2005.

Houle, Michelle E. *Cesar Chavez*. Farmington Hills, MI: Greenhaven Press, 2003.

January, Brendon. *Globalize It!* Minneapolis: Twenty-First Century Books, 2003.

McNeese, Tim. *The Labor Movement: Unionizing America*. New York: Chelsea House, 2007.

Parker, David. *Stolen Dreams: Portrait of Working Children*. Minneapolis: Twenty-First Century Books, 1998.

Roberts, Jeremy. *Franklin D. Roosevelt*. Minneapolis: Twenty-First Century Books, 2003.

Stein, R. Conrad. *The Pullman Strike and the Labor Movement in American History*. Berkeley Heights, NJ: Enslow, 2001.

## WEBSITES

An Eclectic List of Events in U.S. Labor History
http://www.lutins.org/labor.html
This website contains a chronological list of important events in labor history
and links to other sources.

Everything$_2$
http://everything2.com/index.pl?node=Bill%20Haywood
This brief biography of Bill Haywood shows him as a Socialist and union
leader.

The *Time* 100: Walter Reuther
http://www.time.com/time/time100/builder/profile/reuther.html
*Time*'s website of one hundred important people includes a biography of
Walter Reuther.

# PHOTO ACKNOWLEDGMENTS

The images in this book are used with the permission of: IWW and Archives of Labor and Urban Affairs, Wayne State University, pp. 2, 6, 16, 24, 32, 44, 68, 84; Maryland State Archives, p. 7; © SuperStock, Inc./SuperStock, p. 8; The Granger Collection, New York, pp. 10, 21, 42, 54, 71, 72, 80; © Alinari/The Image Works, p. 13; Library of Congress (HAER NO.M1-6-6) background motif though out interior pages, (LC-USZ62-103801) p. 14, (LC-DIG-pga-01282) p. 33, (LC-DIG-ggbain-07131) p. 34, (LC-USZ61-968) p. 35, (LC-USZ61-967) p. 37, (LC-USZ62-40636) p. 38, (LC-USZ62-103849) p. 39, (LC-USZ62-75202) p. 40, (LC-B2-3361-1) p. 45, (LC-DIG-ggbain-10151) p. 48, (LC-USZ62-118677) p. 49, (LC-DIG-ggbain-10241) p. 50, (LC-USZ62-63968) p. 55, (LC-USZ62-7678) p. 58, (LC-USZC4-7860) p. 64, (LC-USZ62-120320) p. 76; © North Wind Picture Archives, pp. 17, 28; © The Lowell Historical Society, p. 18; © Henry Guttmann/Hulton Archive/ Getty Images, p. 19; Humanities and Social Sciences Library/Photography Collection, Miriam and Ira D. Wallach Division of Art, Prints and Photographs, The New York Public Library, Astor, Lenox and Tilden Foundations, p. 20; © The Image Works Archive, p. 22; SECURITY PACIFIC COLLECTION/ Los Angeles Public Library, pp. 25, 90; © Topham/The Image Works, p. 27; Chicago Historical Society, (I03665), p. 30; Idaho State Historial Society, (2005) p. 43, (60-1.1.255), p. 95; © Maurice Branger/Roger-Viollet/The Image Works, p. 57; The Denver Public Library, Western History Collection, (Z-193) p. 59, (X-60505) p. 60, (X-60483) p. 61; HEROLD EXAMINER COLLECTION/ Los Angeles Public Library, pp. 73, 83; AP Photo, pp. 74, 78, 82; AP Photo/ Barry Sweet, p. 85; CSU Archives/Everett Collection/Rex Features USA, p. 86; AP Photo/The Capital Times, Mike DeVries, p. 88; David Pearson/Rex Features USA, p. 89; © David McNew/Getty Images, p. 93.

Front Cover: IWW and Archives of Labor and Urban Affairs, Wayne State University; Back Cover: Library of Congress (HAER NO. MI-6-6).